D1715944

The People Behind CULT MURDERS

The Psychology of Mass Murderers

The People
Behind CULT
MURDERS

Pete Schauer

E | **Enslow Publishing**
101 W. 23rd Street
Suite 240
New York, NY 10011
USA
enslow.com

Published in 2017 by Enslow Publishing, LLC.
101 W. 23rd Street, Suite 240, New York, NY 10011

Library of Congress Cataloging-in-Publication Data
Names: Schauer, Peter J., author.
Title: The people behind cult murders / Pete Schauer.
Description: New York, NY : Enslow Publishing, 2017. | Series: The psychology of mass murderers | Includes bibliographical references and index.
Identifiers: LCCN 2016000209 | ISBN 9780766076105 (library bound)
Subjects: LCSH: Murder—Juvenile literature. | Cults—Juvenile literature. | Murder—Religious aspects—Juvenile literature. | Ritual abuse—Juvenile literature.
Classification: LCC HV6515 .S33 2016 | DDC 364.152/34—dc23
LC record available at http://lccn.loc.gov/2016000209

Printed in the United States of America

To Our Readers: We have done our best to make sure all websites in this book were active and appropriate when we went to press. However, the author and the publisher have no control over and assume no liability for the material available on those websites or on any websites they may link to. Any comments or suggestions can be sent by e-mail to customerservice@enslow.com.

Contents

INTRODUCTION

Murder, defined by *Merriam-Webster's* dictionary, is "the crime of unlawfully killing a person especially with malice aforethought." Unfortunately, it is something that's long been a part of our society. Cults also date back to the beginning of time. Although sometimes but not necessarily involving a religious faith, cults are a small group of people who are devoted to an individual, an idea, an object, a movement, or a type of work.

The earliest cults can be traced back to small groups from European colonies becoming disinterested and upset with members of the church. It wasn't until the twentieth century that cults became more prominent in the United States, as religious authority declined, means of communication increased, and more diverse backgrounds of people came together. This allowed cult leaders to obtain personal followings through mediums like newspapers, radio, television, and mailing lists. The early 1900s were especially crucial

1. *Seeks revenge.* In 30 percent of mass killings, family members are the main victims. The next most likely target is the workplace, to take revenge on a boss or coworkers. Some mass murderers blame society and open fire in public places, or they target police.

2. *Has access to high-powered weapons.* Daniel Nagin, a criminologist at Carnegie Mellon University, says, "It's technologically impossible to kill a lot of people very quickly without access to assault weapons."

3. *Blames other people for his or her problems.*

4. *Often has a mental illness, particularly paranoid schizophrenia.*

5. *Is a loner, with few friends or social connections.*

6. *Carefully plans the attacks, taking days to months to get ready.*

7. *Has suicidal tendencies.*

8. *Has made violent threats, to the target or others indirectly, prior to the attack.*

9. *Is often reacting to a stressor just prior to the rampage, such as the loss of a job or a relationship.*

10. *The actions are not often a surprise to those who know him or her.*

to the development of cults in America. The West Coast saw an influx of immigration, which led to much religious experimentation. Because mainstream religious denominations weren't well established on the West Coast, cults were able to flourish as religious alternatives as well as safe havens for individuals with physical and mental health, who hadn't found faith in mainstream religion. The New Age Movement (NAM)—which is a religious and social movement—was also a big step forward for cults, as the movement derived from Eastern religions saw individuals expand their minds and start to think more openly.

As cults became more prominent in America, so did the violence attributed to some of them, and that violence sometimes involved the act of murder. Perhaps the most infamous murder cult of all time was the Manson family, who formed a cult called "The Family" in 1967. Founded and led by Charles Manson, the Manson family was not a religious cult, although their beliefs did include Scientology and Satanism. The Family committed nine murders over the course of five weeks in the summer of 1969, shaking the state of California and the entire United States to its core.

Prior to Manson's terror, a cult called the "Branch Davidians" formed in 1955. The Davidians, under the leadership of David Koresh, stockpiled an armory of weapons in Waco, Texas, before being raided by the Bureau of Alcohol, Tobacco, and Firearms (ATF) in 1993. The raid led to the death of four ATF agents and about eighty Davidians. What Manson and Koresh both had in common, which are also common traits of cult murder leaders, were that they were manipulative and convincing in getting others to follow their leaders, while also being deranged and oftentimes borderline psychotic. The types of people who follow and join these types of

The People Behind Cult Murders

FBI agents survey the bunker at the Branch Davidian compound that survived the April 19, 1993, fire. Cult leader David Koresh and about eighty of his followers were killed.

cults often feel misguided and misunderstood, and are easy victims for cult leaders because they are given a sense of belonging.

As we move through the different types of murderous cults—which include family, occult and satanic, religious, doomsday, and political and terrorist cults—you'll meet the most prominent cult leaders within each category and the types of people who follow them.

Chapter 1

The Murderous Leaders and Followers of

FAMILY CULTS

Family cults, as the name describes, are cults that are based on a family-like bond between the leader and the followers. While the closest iteration of this type of cult would be for the leader to be related by blood to one follower or multiple followers, not all "family" cults include family members. Leaders of these types of cults create a warm and safe environment for their followers, thus making it feel like they're part of a family. Since trust is a big part of the success of a family cult, it's extremely important that leaders of family cults foster a close-knit environment. In some cases, an intimate—and sometimes sexual—relationship is used to manipulate a follower into doing what the leader wants them to do. Family cult leaders often have an authoritarian control over their followers, and in some cases, it's also totalitarian, with a pyramid system of power in place.

The People Behind Cult Murders

Family cult leaders often instill fear in their followers to keep them loyal and obedient.

These leaders don't want anyone within the cult questioning them or their leadership, and they use fear, intimidation, and manipulation to control their followers. It's important to note that family cults can also be based on other factors, like religion and politics.

Followers of this type of cult have often experienced physical, sexual, and psychological abuse at some point in their life before joining the cult, and may still be experiencing that abuse while in the cult, sometimes even at the mercy of the leader. Because of this, they're easily drawn into joining the cult because it gives them a sense of belonging—a family—which is something they don't currently have but are ultimately seeking. While creating a family environment is important in the beginning—when recruiting members—leaders often resort to fear tactics to keep their followers in line once they've been initiated into the cult. Those fear tactics include everything from self-blame, battering and physical abuse, incest, and induced fear, insecurity, isolation, and deprivation.

Glenn "Taylor" Helzer and Justin Helzer

aka "The Children of Thunder"

Born: Glenn, 1970; Justin, 1972

Occupation: Glenn, stockbroker; Justin, cable installer

Diagnosis: Justin, shared psychological disorder

Arrested: August 7, 2000

Died: Justin, April 14, 2013

Brothers Glenn Helzer (who went by his middle name, Taylor,) and Justin Helzer were raised in a Mormon family just northeast of San Francisco, California. Family, friends, and coworkers state that the boys had a normal upbringing. However, none of them could have predicted what the Helzer boys—who eventually became known as "The Children of Thunder"—were capable of. After graduating from high school, the brothers fulfilled their Mormon requirement, completing two years in the mission field in separate locations and returning to California for work. Taylor accepted a job as a stockbroker at Morgan Stanley Dean Witter while Justin found work as a cable installer. In 1993, Taylor married a woman, Anne, with whom he had two daughters. The couple separated three years later when Taylor's personality started to change and he decided he was tired of being a good Mormon and a good husband. Taylor began abusing drugs and

Glenn Helzer is shown in a police photo taken in Martinez, California, on August 25, 2000.

alcohol and was kicked out of the Mormon Church. Around this time, Taylor started to formulate his own religious beliefs and believed that he was a prophet who could receive messages directly from God. After receiving a disability leave from his job as a stockbroker, Taylor became more and more disillusioned in his own prophecy.

In 1999, the brothers attended a murder mystery dinner at a Mormon temple where they met Dawn Godman, a suicidal outcast, who started dating the younger brother, Justin. The brothers let Godman in on their religious beliefs. They spent four days in a windowless room to confront their inner demons, planning to defeat Satan by starting a self-help group and taking over the Mormon Church by assassinating church leaders. To fund the self-help group, Taylor came up with a scheme to extort money from and kill an ex-client. To complete the plan, Taylor's new girlfriend, Selina Bishop, whom he met at a rave in spring 2000, would be the one to open a checking account and cash the stolen checks. It was all falling into place for the Helzer brothers. Carrying out their plan, the Helzer brothers went to the home of Ivan and Annette Stineman on July 30, 2000. They abducted these ex-clients of Taylor, drugged them, and forced them to write out two checks worth $100,000, made payable to Selina Bishop. The brothers then killed the senior couple, with Justin bashing Ivan Stineman's head against the tile floor until he died, and Taylor slitting Annette's throat with a hunting knife. The next day, the brothers used a power saw to cut the bodies into pieces and stuffed them into gym bags filled with rocks. They planned to dump the bodies in a river.

After Bishop cashed the checks for them, the brothers looked to tie up their loose ends. They murdered Bishop with a hammer on August 2 and then Bishop's mother, Jennifer Villarin, and her

Carma Helzer leans back into her husband, Gerry Helzer, during a media conference in Concord, California, on August 10, 2000. They are the parents of Glenn and Justin Helzer.

boyfriend, James Gamble. Selina Bishop had made the mistake of telling her mother about the brothers and the bank account, so the brothers killed Villarin because she knew about them, and unfortunately Gamble was an innocent witness. Taylor shot the couple using a gun that Justin had bought in his own name.

Following these two murders, police quickly connected all five of the killings to the Helzer brothers and arrested them and Dawn—for her role as an accomplice—on August 7, 2000. Police were able to catch "The Children of Thunder" by connecting multiple puzzle pieces: the Stineman's daughter's reporting her parents missing, Bishop failing to show up for work and reporting her missing, and Stineman's abandoned car, containing a chainsaw and sawhorse with Justin and Godman's fingerprints on them (found in an Oakland neighborhood). In 2005, both brothers were sentenced to death for their roles in the five murders. Godman received a thirty-seven-year sentence after testifying against the brothers in exchange for a prison sentence that didn't include the death penalty. On April 14, 2013, Justin committed suicide by hanging himself with a bedsheet in his jail cell.[1]

Psychological red flags:

Belief of prophecy

Pattern of cult violence:

Beating, stabbing, and shooting

Number of victims:

Five

Born: **May 3, 1950**

Occupation: **Self-proclaimed prophet, minister, and tour guide**

Arrested: **January 7, 1990**

Died: **October 24, 2006**

Growing up in Missouri, Jeffrey Lundgren was a member of the RLDS Church, better known as the Reorganized Church of Jesus Christ of Latter Day Saints. According to his neighbors, Lundgren was abused by his father as a child. However, Lundgren spent more time with his father as he got older, with his father teaching him how to hunt and wield a gun. Little did his father know that the hunting trips with his son would influence Jeffrey's future as a cult murderer.

When it came time for college, Lundgren attended Central Missouri State University.[2] He visited an RLDS house frequently, where he met his future wife, Alice Keeler. Keeler was also abused by her father when she was a child, and the two formed a strong bond. It wasn't long before Lundgren and Keeler were married in 1970, and by 1979, the couple had three children. Lundgren was a lay minister with the RLDS as well as a tour guide for the Kirtland Temple in Ohio, a historic worship building for the RLDS. It was at this time that Lundgren developed a following—a cult of followers— as he began to teach a type of interpretation of scripture. Although he didn't come up with the concept, Lundgren proclaimed to his followers that he had, manipulating members of his cult to further buy into his views. He continued to build his following within the

Murder victims Dennis Avery and his wife, Cheryl, are shown in a family portrait with their daughters *(left to right)*, Tina, Karen, and Rebecca.

RLDS, but he was fired from his job as a tour guide within the church in 1987 on suspicion of theft.

Following his removal, Lundgren moved his family to a farmhouse in Ohio, where members of his cult moved in with him and his family. He broke away from the RLDS and became more controlling and manipulative of his followers, forbidding them to speak to each other and telling them it was a sin to do so. He eavesdropped on cult members so that they believed he could read their minds.

Lundgren and his cult began plotting to take over the Kirtland Temple, for what Lundgren referred to as "the second coming," which involved burglarizing the homes around the church and committing murder. As more cult members began living in the farmhouse, more suspicion grew from neighbors that there was a cult in their town. The Kirtland Police learned of the takeover plot, and the Federal Bureau of Investigation (FBI) launched a domestic terrorism investigation against Lundgren and his cult after two FBI informants came forward and detailed Lundgren's plans.

At this point, seven of the twelve cult members were living with Lundgren and his family in the farmhouse. The Avery family, consisting of husband Dennis and his wife, Cheryl, and their three daughters were the only members not living with the cult. Lundgren felt that the Averys were living in sin and lacked faith by not residing with the rest of the cult, and in addition to that, felt disrespected that the Averys weren't giving all of their money to him and the rest of his followers. Because of that, Lundgren decided that the Averys needed to be killed for their disloyalty. On April 17, 1989, Lundgren invited the Avery family for dinner. He led each member of the family out to a barn individually, where each was

Jeffrey Lundgren shot the Avery family in this barn near Kirtland, Ohio.

bound, gagged, and shot to death with a .45 caliber gun. Each body was placed into a pit that members of the cult had previously dug.[3]

It wasn't until nine months later, on January 7, 1990, that Lundgren, his wife, and his son Damon were arrested for their parts in the Avery murders. Ten other members of the cult had already been arrested. Alice and Damon were both sentenced to life in prison, and Jeffrey received the death penalty and was executed by lethal injection in Ohio on October 24, 2006.

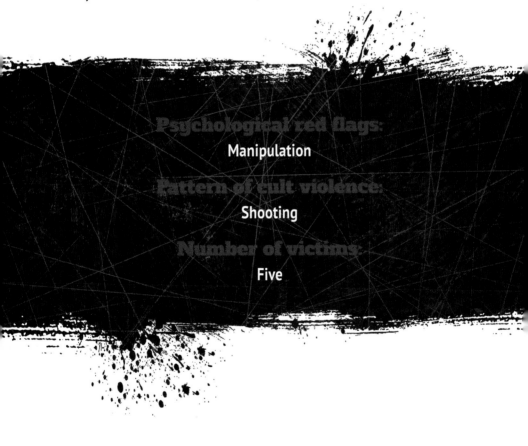

Psychological red flags:

Manipulation

Pattern of cult violence:

Shooting

Number of victims:

Five

Ron and Dan Lafferty

Born: Ron, November 4, 1941; Dan, 1948

Arrested: August 1984

In 1984, brothers Ron and Dan Lafferty committed an unthinkable crime against their own family. Ron and his younger brother Dan subscribed to a fundamentalist version of Mormonism and were members of a radical polygamous group, the "School of Prophets." This led them to grow their hair long and believe that they were prophets. Clearly delusional, the two brothers murdered their sister-in-law, Brenda Lafferty, and her fifteen-month old baby, Erica, on July 24, 1984. What was the reason for these murders? Brenda wouldn't join her husband's radical polygamous cult. Brenda was married to Allen, Dan and Ron's youngest brother. In addition to Brenda not wanting to join the cult, the brothers believed that Brenda had influenced Ron's wife to leave him after she didn't allow him to have another wife. Those two factors led to her and her daughter's gruesome murder. The two brothers slit the throats of their two victims with a ten-inch (twenty-five centimeter) boning knife.[4] Dan, who believed himself to be the prophet Elijah, said that he received a revelation from God and that he instructed him and his brother to kill Brenda and her daughter.

As a result of the two murders, the two brothers were charged and tried separately for the homicides. Dan represented himself during the trial, despite having access to a standby counsel, and when he was found guilty, he received a sentence of five years to life, which was upheld by the Utah Supreme Court. Although he tried to kill himself while incarcerated in the Utah County jail in December 1984, Ron was found competent for trial by Utah State Hospital doctors, and his sentencing of the death penalty was upheld in the Utah Supreme Court. The 10th Circuit Court of Appeals went on to overturn the lower court's ruling, saying that it was an error that Ron was found competent to attend trial. After receiving treatment in the Utah State Hospital and seeing three years pass by, Ron was again tried for the homicides after his competency was restored, and in 1996, he was found guilty of the capital offense and is currently on death row.

Unfortunately, that's not where the story ends for deaths tied to the Lafferty brothers. While in prison, Dan often received visits from Kristi Strack and her husband, Benjamin. Kristi was only six when Dan and Ron committed the murders, but she grew obsessed with the case and with Dan, which led to a lengthy friendship while Dan was incarcerated. In 2003, author Jon Krakauer wrote a book about the murders committed by Dan and Ron, titled *Under the Banner of Heaven*, with which Kristi was also obsessed. Kristi reached out to Dan's daughter, who was able to make the connection between Dan and Kristi, which grew quite close, with it being said that the two were in love, despite Kristi's marriage to Benjamin and Benjamin's fondness of Dan. Throughout the friendship, Dan even believed he was able to cure Kristi of her ovarian cancer, because of his prophecy.

The Strack family, who had suffered from addiction problems for years, had their ties cut with Dan in 2008 when Kristi tried to pass her brother off as Benjamin so that he could visit Dan in

Ron Lafferty, center, is escorted out of the Utah County Court House by Utah County Sheriff Deputies after the first day of jury selection in his murder trial on April 25, 1985, in Provo, Utah.

prison. Authorities at the prison revoked Kristi's access, and contact between Dan and Kristi ended. Shortly after, Kristi and Benjamin pleaded guilty to forgery charges and disorderly conduct, part of their criminal history that dated back twelve years.

Possibly having shared Dan's twisted beliefs, the Stracks, who often spoke to family and friends about wanting to escape the world because of the growing evil within it, committed

Dan Lafferty, shown here in Utah State Prison in 2003, thought he was a prophet.

suicide. Their three children, ages fourteen, twelve, and eleven, also died. Kristi and Benjamin were found with red liquid next to their bodies. The children were discovered on and near a bed, with empty bottles of liquid methadone and cold and flu medicine next to them. Benjamin's body contained high levels of heroin. Kristi's body tested positive for methadone, dextrorphan, diphenhydramine, and doxylamine. Both of their deaths were ruled as suicides. The two youngest children's deaths were ruled homicides—likely killed by their parents. Investigators don't believe that the Stracks got their beliefs from Dan, and the Strack family's deaths were never legally or officially tied to Dan.

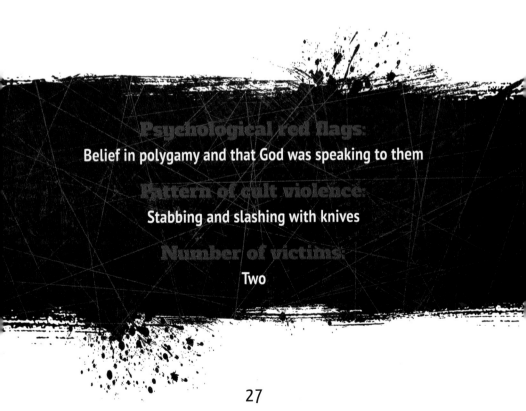

Psychological red flags:

Belief in polygamy and that God was speaking to them

Pattern of cult violence:

Stabbing and slashing with knives

Number of victims:

Two

Charles Manson
aka "Charlie Manson"

Born: **November 12, 1934**

Occupation: **Singer/songwriter**

Diagnosis: **Schizophrenia and paranoid delusional disorder**

Arrested: **October 12, 1969**

When discussing serial killers, cult murders, or just murder in general, it's nearly impossible to have a conversation without mentioning Charles Manson and "The Family." Manson was born in Cincinnati, Ohio, in 1934, and it's believed that he never knew his biological father, Colonel Walker Scott. He was born to a single mother, sixteen-year-old Kathleen Maddox, and was initially called "no name Maddox" before becoming Charles Milles Maddox a few weeks later. Following the birth of Charles, Kathleen married William Manson, and gave Charles her new husband's last name. Further details of Manson's upbringing and childhood are in dispute due to the fact that Manson has provided interviewers with a variety of different stories. One of those stories states that his mother, for a pitcher of beer, once sold him to a waitress who had no children, and that Manson's uncle retrieved him back a few days later.[5]

Manson's home life was unstable. His mother and uncle spent five years in prison for robbing a gas station in West Virginia when he was a boy, forcing him to be placed under the care of his aunt and another uncle.[6] Manson considers his sole happy childhood

Charles Manson and his murderous cult, The Family, are responsible for killing nine people.

memory the time when his mother embraced him on the day she was released from prison. Kathleen eventually tried to have Charles placed in a foster home, but that was denied, and Charles was placed by the courts in the Gibault School for Boys in Indiana. From there, Manson went on to commit a slew of crimes, which included the burgling of a liquor store and other armed robberies of stores, various break-ins, and motor vehicle theft that put him in and out of prisons and correctional facilities. It wasn't until the release from his second imprisonment that Manson began to form his murderous cult, The Family, after moving to San Francisco in 1967.

During his time spent in prison, Manson studied Scientology and borrowed philosophy from the Process Church, which believed that both Satan and Christ would join forces at the end of the world to make a judgment on humanity. He began exuding his beliefs upon a group of followers—mostly made of women—and taught them that they were the reincarnation of the original Christian faith and that the Romans were the establishment. Manson believed in the notion of "Helter Skelter," a title he appropriated from the song by the Beatles.[7] His belief was that there was a race war coming, and that murder would immediately help to end that war. What ensued from here were a string of nine murders committed by Manson and The Family during five weeks in the summer of 1969. Actress Sharon Tate and coffee heiress Abigail Folger were two of The Family's most notable victims, in addition to Leno LaBianca, a prominent supermarket executive, and his wife, Rosemary.

On October 12, 1969, Manson, along with other members of The Family, was arrested on grand theft auto charges. While incarcerated, authorities learned of Manson's connections to multiple murders. On December 5, Manson and other members of his cult

From left to right, Patricia Krenwinkel, Susan Atkins, and Leslie Van Houten were found guilty of the murders of actress Sharon Tate and six other people, in collaboration with Charles Manson.

The People Behind Cult Murders

were indicted for the murders of Sharon Tate and her friends as well as the LaBianca murders. Following the trial, all Tate-LaBianca defendants, including Manson, were found guilty of first-degree murder. Their conviction occurred despite the fact that defense attorney Ronald Hughes failed to show up in court and was never seen again, which led to speculation that he was murdered by The Family to keep Manson and other members of the cult out of trouble.

Manson was originally sentenced to the death penalty, but the California Supreme Court found the penalty to be unconstitutional and changed Manson's sentence to life in prison, where he currently resides.

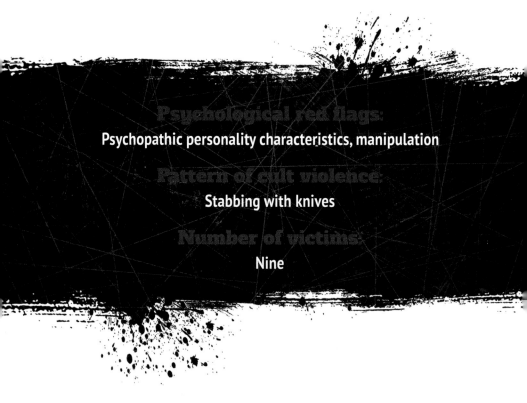

Psychological red flags:

Psychopathic personality characteristics, manipulation

Pattern of cult violence:

Stabbing with knives

Number of victims:

Nine

Chapter 2

The Murderous Leaders and Followers of

OCCULT AND SATANIC CULTS

Satanic cults—as you might have guessed—revolve around various beliefs in the devil, or Satan, and typically result in the acts of satanic ritual abuse (SRA), which includes murder. SRA is also known as ritual abuse, organized abuse, and sadistic ritual abuse. It was somewhat popularized in the 1980s, during the McMartin preschool trial, in which a family who ran a preschool was criminally charged for various sexual acts against children.[1] In more extreme cases, children were abducted and bred for sacrifice, pornography, and prostitution as part of satanic cults.[2] Occultism is the belief in something supernatural, often magical or divinatory. In occults, the leader is able to manipulate his or her followers by getting them to believe that they have magical or supernatural powers, holding that over them as they participate in illegal activities for, or alongside, the leader. Both of these types of cults are usually led by a leader who mesmerizes people with his charm and devotions. With this false sense of camaraderie, cult members band together as a force against the outside world. They are often clandestine and form their own private communes.

The types of people who join cults are often those who are seeking acceptance and want a deeper experience in the divine. Experts who have studied satanic cults have found that many followers are extremely intelligent and well educated. Sometimes, people who have been disappointed by traditional religion will find the acceptance they need in a cult. In the satanic cult, the leader is supreme and is the only connection to the world and eternity. After they have been slowly brainwashed, followers close themselves away from the rest of the world and look to their leader for everything. These people are often abused physically, mentally, and sexually in order to break their individual wills. The only loyalties they have are to the cult and to the leader. They are often convinced to do illegal things if it benefits the group. Those who dare break any of the rules are severely punished.

Members of satanic cults are taught to avoid the outside world and all it has to offer. They are compelled to sever ties with family and friends and to take on a new identity. Since cult leaders usually suffer from extreme delusions and paranoia, they teach their followers that the world around them is evil and is trying to destroy everything they hold as sacred. Satanic cults are often hostile to any outside interference and view the government as a threat. While most satanic cults keep to themselves and are not much of a threat to society, many of them practice abuse that is so terrible that the

Members of satanic cults worship Satan and engage in ritual abuse.

government has to intervene. Sometimes, it ends up in the loss of lives from both sides. Whether a cult claims a satanic background or worships a spiritual being that is traditionally good, totalitarian leadership and member abuse never benefits anyone in the end.

Adolfo Costanzo
aka "The Godfather of Matamoros"

Born: **November 1, 1962**

Occupation: **Tarot card reader and magician**

Died: **May 6, 1989**

Adolfo de Jesus Constanzo was born in Miami, Florida, to a widowed Cuban immigrant, Delia Aurora Gonzalex del Valle. She had two more children, both fathered by different men. After her first husband died, Delia remarried and moved to San Juan, Puerto Rico, where Adolfo was born, baptized Roman Catholic, and influenced by Delia's participation in Palo Mayombe, a religion developed in the Spanish Empire that involves the sacrificing of animals. The family moved back to Miami in 1972, where Adolfo's stepfather passed away. Delia remarried a man who was involved in the local drug trade and the occult, and she and Adolfo were both arrested numerous times for theft, vandalism, and shoplifting. It was clear to see from a young age that Adolfo was bound to lead a life of crime.

After graduating from high school, Adolfo took up with a Haitian Palo Mayombe priest—also a sorcerer—who taught Adolfo many skills tied to the sacrificing of animals, drug dealing, and being a con artist. Adolfo's mother believed her son had special powers; she claimed that Adolfo predicted the attempted assassination of Ronald Reagan in 1981.

The People Behind Cult Murders

As an adult, Costanzo relocated to Mexico City, where he met Martin Quintana, Jorge Montes, and Omar Orea, who eventually became his followers in his cult. Costanzo and his followers started a business casting spells that were said to bring good luck. The rituals included the sacrificing of chickens, snakes, zebras, goats, and lion cubs. Constanzo started to get mixed up into the drug game, as a lot of his clients were drug dealers and corrupt cops who liked the violence that came with Costanzo's "magical" spells. As he got deeper and deeper into his magic, Costanzo started using human bones in his *nganga*, or cauldron. He started raiding grave-yards to support his spells.[3] As he became more confident in his magic, Costanzo started to believe that his magic was the reason why the drug cartels were so successful, and thus he demanded that he be named a partner with one of the most powerful and corrupt families in the area, the Calzadas. When the Calzadas rejected Costanzo's demand, seven family members turned up dead, with fingers, toes, ears, brains, and even a spine found missing—likely used for his nganga.

After his deal with the Calzadas fell through, Costanzo cozied up to another cartel, the Hernandez brothers, and moved to Rancho Santa Elena, a desert compound in Mexico. There, he committed more sadistic ritual murders. One of those murders took place on March 13, 1989, when members of Constanzo's cult abducted premed student Mark Kilroy from outside of a bar in Mexico. They killed him at the cult's ranch. Police investigated Kilroy's disappearance and discovered the cult through an unrelated drug investigation. The police raided the ranch and connected Kilroy's murder to the cult. They dug up Kilroy's dismembered body and fourteen other bodies at the ranch. After fleeing to Mexico City with four of his followers,

Five people arrested in connection with the deaths of fifteen people whose bodies were found on a ranch in northern Mexico stand by a table filled with satanic cult items found in an apartment where they were captured, May 7, 1989, in Mexico City. They are Maria del Rocio Cuevas Guerra; Alvaro de Leon, who said he killed cult leader Adolfo de Jesus Costanzo when police arrived; Omar Orea; Maria de Lourdes Bueno Lopez; and Sara Aldrete, a former honor student at a Texas college and Constanzo's companion.

The People Behind Cult Murders

Constanzo was located by the police. Surrounded and determined not to go to jail, Constanzo ordered his follower, Alvaro de Leon, to shoot both him and Quintana. All in all, a total of fourteen members of the cult were arrested and charged with multiple crimes, and sentenced to a slew prison time.

Psychological red flags:

Practice of Palo Mayombe, belief in magic, and association with drug cartels

Pattern of cult violence:

Shooting, and stabbing with a machete

Number of victims:

At least twenty-five

Carl Drew
aka "Son of Satan"

> **Born: 1954**
> **Occupation: Pimp**
> **Arrested: April 1980**

Carl Drew was both a pimp and satanic cult leader. He was a self-proclaimed devil worshipper in Fall River, Massachusetts, in the 1970s to the early 1980s. Like other cult leaders, Drew held meetings with his followers during which they engaged in devil-worshipping chants and ritualistic sacrifices. Drew's first victim, Donna Levesque, was found with her body mutilated on October 13, 1979.

Levesque's body was found behind the bleachers of a vocational high school, with her hands bound behind her back and her head beaten in with a rock. There was also evidence of sexual assault. There were two witnesses to the murder: prostitutes Karen Marsden and Robin Murphy. Reports stated that Murphy started as an observer and moved to become a participant, but Marsden resisted Drew's sadistic cult rituals and sought to break away from his control.

Four months later, on February 8, 1980, Drew and his cult murdered Marsden as part of a sacrifice. They first tortured her by ripping out her hair and fingernails. They beat her over the head with stones before Drew snapped her neck. In a fit of rage, Drew's satanic beliefs took over, and he deployed Murphy to slit Marsden's throat, and she obliged. Drew then removed Marsden's head and

Donna Levesque, Carl Drew's first victim, was discovered behind a set of high school bleachers.

gave it to his followers, who kicked it around like a football.[4] Drew smeared Marsden's blood on Murphy's forehead.

On April 13, 1980, fragments of Marsden's skull and pieces of her clothing were found in the woods, and authorities were able to match the few skull fragments to an X-ray of Marsden's skull that was taken in 1978 when she was treated for a sinus issue. By this time, Murphy's conscience had grown guilty, and she cracked under the pressure of hiding Drew's two murders, which she had witnessed. She told authorities that Drew was the killer responsible for the two murders.

For her role in Marsden's death, Murphy accepted a life sentence, but had that knocked down when she agreed to testify against Drew for the state. Murphy was paroled in 2004; however, she violated parole in 2011 and was sent back to prison.

At the age of twenty-six, Drew was indicted for Levesque's murder on March 3, 1981. In the meantime, he was mentioned in court proceedings against Andre Maltais, an ex-boyfriend of Murphy's, who was convicted for the murder of prostitute Barbara Raposa. It's suspected that Drew also committed the murder of Raposa, but he was never tried or convicted for her murder.[5] Ten days later, Drew was convicted for Marsden's murder and sentenced to life in prison. An additional ten years was tacked onto his sentence when he was convicted for assaulting a prostitute with a deadly weapon.

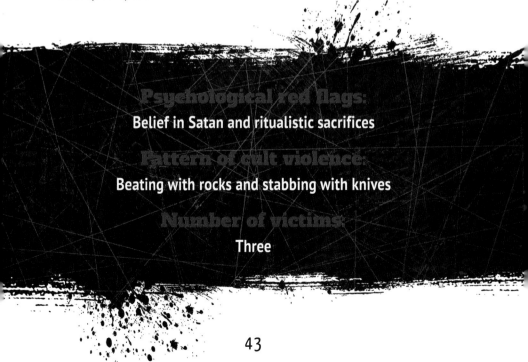

Psychological red flags:

Belief in Satan and ritualistic sacrifices

Pattern of cult violence:

Beating with rocks and stabbing with knives

Number of victims:

Three

Robin Gecht

aka "The Chicago Rippers" and "The Ripper Crew"

Born: November 30, 1953

Arrested: October 20, 1982

Robin Gecht was the leader of "The Ripper Crew," a satanic cult that was also made up of Edward Spreitzer, Andrew Kokoraleis, and Thomas Kokoraleis. Gecht was thirty years old when the cult began murdering; as the oldest member he was the natural leader (Spreitzer was only twenty-one and the Kokoraleis brothers were just teenagers). Not much is known about Gecht's early life, but it is said that he once worked for John Wayne Gacy, a fellow serial killer.[6] Led by Gecht, The Ripper Crew, or "The Chicago Rippers," targeted young women as part of their satanic cult rituals.

The crew drove in a van, looking for prostitutes to sacrifice in Gecht's apartment. In one of the more sadistic rituals, Gecht and his fellow cult members removed the left breast from each victim. They continued to assault the body, and even eat some of it, as they read passages from *The Satanic Bible*. The rituals took place at an altar in the attic of Gecht's home, where the cult gathered after Gecht's wife left for work at night.

Linda Sutton was the cult's first victim in the spring of 1981. The cult raped and murdered her behind the Brer Rabbit Hotel, which was an area where prostitutes hung out. From that point

The Ripper Crew drove around town in a van, looking for their next victim.

on, Gecht and The Ripper Crew terrorized the city of Chicago in 1981 and 1982, committing some of the most brutal and heinous crimes in US history. The cult's last victim, a teenage prostitute, survived the attack and was able to identify Gecht's van. Meanwhile, Spreitzer turned himself in and provided a full confession to the authorities, resulting in the arrest of the other three members. Unfortunately, the authorities never had enough evidence to connect Gecht to the murders, but he was arrested on October 20, 1982, and sentenced to 120 years in prison for the mutilation and rape of an eighteen-year-old prostitute. As far as his companions go, Andrew Kokoraleis and Edwards Spreitzer were sentenced to death, and Thomas Kokoraleis was sentenced with life in prison for killing Lorraine Borowski.

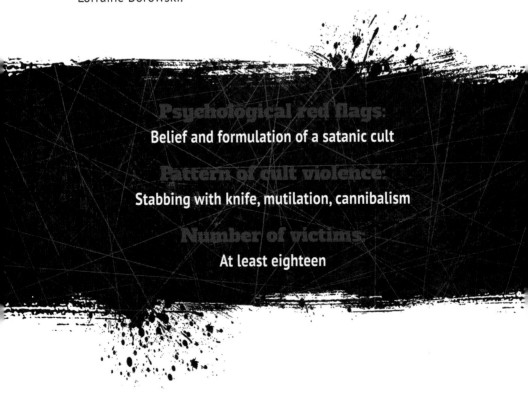

Psychological red flags:

Belief and formulation of a satanic cult

Pattern of cult violence:

Stabbing with knife, mutilation, cannibalism

Number of victims:

At least eighteen

Richard Ramirez

aka "The Night Stalker," "The Walk-In Killer," and "The Valley Intruder"

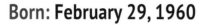

Born: **February 29, 1960**

Occupation: **Burglar**

Arrested: **August 31, 1985**

Died: **June 7, 2013**

Richard Ramirez, most commonly referred to as "The Night Stalker," was one of the most prolific murderers of the late twentieth century. While Ramirez didn't lead a cult or have any followers, he did hold a strong belief in Satan and satanic rituals, incorporating this belief and those acts into his murders. Born in Texas, Ramirez was the youngest of five children and was often physically abused by his father as a child. The young Ramirez looked up to his older cousin, Miguel, who was a Green Beret in the US Army. Miguel would share stories from his days of combat, even sharing photos of victims he had killed and Vietnamese women whom he had raped. Miguel also taught his cousin skills he had learned in the military, including how to stealthily kill. Ramirez was present when Miguel shot and killed his wife during a domestic dispute in 1973.

Roberto, Ramirez's brother-in-law, who was a "peeping Tom," also had an influence on the young man. Ramirez accompanied Roberto on his sexual-peeking escapades. Around this time, Ramirez

Serial killer Richard Ramirez was booked and photographed on December 12, 1984, in Los Angeles, California.

began using the hallucinogenic drug lysergic acid diethylamide (LSD) and developed an interest in Satanism.

Ramirez got a job at a Holiday Inn, where he robbed sleeping customers. Ramirez was quickly fired from the position when a customer returned to his room and caught Ramirez attempting to rape his wife. The furious husband beat Ramirez, but the out-of-state couple refused to return to Texas to testify, so Ramirez was never convicted of criminal charges. Shortly after this, twenty-two-year-old Ramirez moved to California and began his murderous rampages. Ramirez's first murder occurred in April 1984, when a nine-year-old was found raped, beaten, and stabbed to death, hanging from a pipe in a hotel basement in San Francisco.[7] From there, Ramirez went on a spree of killings from June 1984 to August 1985. His typical process was to break into a home at night, kill the husband, and rape and kill the wife. His most common method of murder included shooting and stabbing his victims, and Ramirez often left a pentagram—a sign of devil worship—at the scene of his crimes as a calling card.

The capture of "The Night Stalker" started when he was seen by thirteen-year-old James Romero III. Romero III was the neighbor of Bill Carns and Inez Erickson, victims of a Ramirez attack. The teenager wrote down the partial license plate of a stolen Toyota that Ramirez was traveling in, and Erickson, who survived the attack, was able to give a description of Ramirez. The police immediately released a photo of Ramirez to the public. After attempting multiple carjackings to escape authorities, Ramirez was subdued by Los Angeles residents, who recognized him and stopped him from stealing another car. One of the residents struck Ramirez over the head with a metal pipe, and residents were able to hold Ramirez until police arrived and brought him into custody.

On September 20, 1989, Ramirez was convicted of multiple charges, including thirteen counts of murder, five attempted murders, eleven sexual assaults, and fourteen burglaries. Ramirez's high-profile trial cost $1.8 million, the most expensive trial in the history of California prior to O.J. Simpson's murder trial in 1994. During this time, Ramirez married his wife, Doreen Lioy, a "fan" who had been writing him letters and visiting him in prison. The two married in San Quentin State Prison in California on October 3, 1996, but eventually separated.[8] Ramirez was sentenced to death on November 7, 1989, but he never made it to the gas chamber, as he died on June 7, 2013 from complications of blood cancer.

Psychological red flags:

Belief and obsession with Satan

Pattern of cult violence:

Shooting, stabbing, and beating

Number of victims:

Thirteen

Nicola Sapone
aka "The Beasts of Satan"

> Born: **January 28, 1977**
> Occupation: **Musician**
> Arrested: **2004**

Nicola Sapone was the leader of an Italian heavy metal band and murderous satanic cult called "Beasts of Satan," in the late 1990s to early 2000s. Not much is known about Sapone or his fellow band/cult mates' early life, so the story starts in the late 1990s, when Sapone and his satanic cult began killing.

The Beasts of Satan's first murder was a double homicide in January 1998 near Somma Lombardo, Italy. Sapone and fellow cult members Andrea Volpe and Mario Maccione killed two of their band mates, nineteen-year-old Chiara Marino and sixteen-year-old Fabio Tollis, in what was called a "drug-fueled satanic sacrifice."[9] Marino and Tollis had spent the night drinking and listening to heavy metal music at Midnight, a heavy metal rock club in the city. Sapone, Volpe, and Maccione lured them into the woods and stabbed their two friends to death, also striking Tollis in the head with a hammer. It's reported that the three then buried the dead bodies in a grave in the woods and celebrated by dancing over the dead bodies, screaming and laughing.[10]

Prior to killing Tollis, Sapone forced the young boy to call his father and tell him that he would not be home that night and would

On June 21, 2005, Nicola Sapone, left, was escorted by two Italian police officers as he entered court for a hearing of the Beasts of Satan killings.

be spending the night with his girlfriend. Michele Tollis, Fabio's father, didn't fully believe the story, but unfortunately he could not prevent his son's murder. After learning of the band's involvement in Satanism and the occult, Michele spent the next six years building a file against the band and individuals he believed were responsible for his son's death.

Their third and final murder wasn't committed until January 2004—six years later—when Volpe killed his ex-girlfriend, twenty-seven-year-old Mariangela Pezzotta. Believing that Pezzotta knew too much about the band's satanic beliefs and the murders of Marino and Tollis, Volpe invited Pezzotta for a "friendly" dinner, shot her, and then buried her alive in a greenhouse near Somma Lombardo with the help of his current girlfriend, eighteen-year-old Elisabetta Ballarin. After killing Pezzotta, Volpe and Ballarin had to get rid of her car, the remaining evidence. The couple got high on cocaine and heroin before trying to dump the car in a river; they crashed the car and were arrested.

After learning of the third murder, Michele Tollis went to the police with his file on the cult. Mr. Tollis's file—combined with Volpe's willingness to help in exchange for leniency—helped lead the police to the two buried bodies of Marino and Tollis. As the investigation continued, Maccione confessed to beating Tollis to death with a hammer, and thus Maccione was taken into police custody.

Prior to the first murder, members of the Beasts of Satan were accused of pushing Andrea Bontade, the band's drummer, to commit suicide because he had refused to help the cult kill Marino and Tollis in a previous plot. Bontade wound up drinking heavily and committing suicide by crashing his car. The cult was looked at by the police, but no charges were ever brought upon them.

The three murders were more than enough evidence for authorities, though. On February 22, 2005, Volpe was sentenced to thirty years in prison, and fellow cult member Pietro Guerrieri was sentenced to sixteen years. Four other members of the cult, Paolo Leoni, Maco Zampollo, Eros Monterosso, and Elisabetta Ballarin all received lengthy sentences between twenty-four and twenty-six years for their participation in the three murders.

Sapone, the leader of the cult and the person who was thought to be the organizer behind all of the murders, received a life sentence. These heinous murders occurred at a time when Satanism and the occult were a growing attraction in Italy. As a result of the murders, priest Don Aldo Buonaito attempted to have death metal music banned in Italy, but he was unsuccessful.

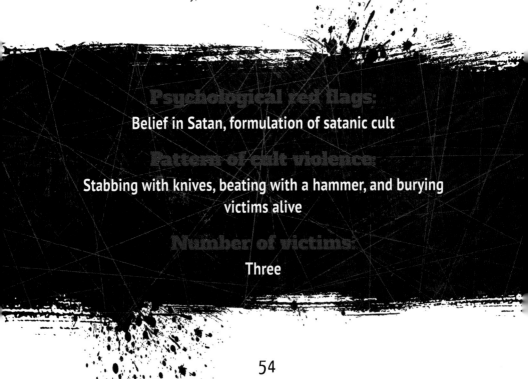

Psychological red flags:

Belief in Satan, formulation of satanic cult

Pattern of cult violence:

Stabbing with knives, beating with a hammer, and burying victims alive

Number of victims:

Three

The Murderous Leaders and Followers of

RELIGIOUS CULTS

Historically, there are religious cults, such as "The People's Temple of the Disciples of Christ," that have helped drive popularity of this type of cult. The People's Temple of the Disciples of Christ, which was also known as the "People's Temple," was a religious cult founded by Jim Jones in 1955 that resulted in a mass suicide in Guyana in 1978. Some religious cults are focused on unified hate toward a particular religion or portion of the population, while others are focused on an end goal, such as a mass suicide, for a reason only fully understood by the leader, as in the case of the People's Temple.

Religious cults are typically formed by incredibly charismatic individuals who form their own reality and strive for power. Sometimes the belief comes from a delusion that could be attributed to a lack of realistic grounding; alternately, there could be a hidden

Dead bodies lie around the compound of the People's Temple cult on November 18, 1978, after the over nine hundred members of the cult, led by Reverend Jim Jones, died from drinking cyanide-laced Kool-Aid. They were victims of the largest mass suicide in modern history.

agenda, as could be thought of with the church of Scientology, in which they tend to focus a lot of effort on gaining wealth.[1] Cults can have slightly varying belief systems, however. They typically revolve around one leader's attempt to gain more members while believing that he knows about a religious reality that most of the world is ignorant of. This is why, in some occurrences, these cults often commit mass suicides, because they feel they're acting on specific orders and religious beliefs from the cult leader. Also, because there is typically only one leader, his or her word can be taken as "gospel" at times.

These cults have very rigid structures. The leader will constantly reinforce how much the followers need this group to thrive. Typically, followers won't have access to the outside world; however, this isn't always the case. The purpose of cutting them off from technology and socializing with outsiders is that it's supposed to prevent any potential critical thinking that may lead them to question their leader or his/her beliefs. The group will have only one leader. The leader will usually have a close circle of trusted individuals who share the same vision, but they won't be revered in the same regard. There is a strong hierarchical structure to the group, and when followers are hooked, it is usually up to them to bring more recruits. This both reinforces their belief as well as helps them feel like they are contributing to a higher cause.

The relationship that these cults have with the outside world is usually strained. The leader will put on a front when associating with the outside world, and the followers will likely regard outsiders with a mentality of "either you're with us or you're against us," which will be passed down from the start of the recruitment.

Marshall Applewhite
aka "Bo" and "Do"

Born: May 17, 1931
Occupation: Music teacher
Died: March 1997

As the son of a Presbyterian minister, Marshall Herff Applewhite was religious from the start, especially during his days as a student at Corpus Christi High School and Austin College in Texas. After receiving a bachelor's degree in 1952 in psychology, he studied at Union Presbyterian Seminary to become a minister. During his time at the seminary, Applewhite decided to switch gears and pursue a music career. He left the seminary and became the music director of a North Carolina Presbyterian church.

Applewhite was also a baritone singer and a fan of George Frideric Handel's musical compositions. Applewhite's music career was put on hold in 1954 when he was drafted by the army and sent to serve in Austria and New Mexico in the US Army Signal Corps. After two years in the service, he left the military and earned a master's degree in music at the University of Colorado.[2]

Shortly after receiving his degree in music, Applewhite moved to New York City, hoping to make it big as a professional singer. That proved unsuccessful, and he accepted a teaching position at the University of Alabama. Applewhite was fired for attempting to have a sexual relationship with a male student. He became frustrated with his sexual thoughts and desires, especially because his religion did not support same-sex relationships.[3] Separating from his wife as a result of the relationship in 1965, Applewhite divorced his wife three years later. Now single and on his own, he relocated to Houston, Texas, to teach at the University of St. Thomas. Applewhite also served as chair of the music department and the choral director of an Episcopal church nearby.

Despite being openly gay at this point, Applewhite still pursued a relationship with a younger woman. However, after feeling pressure from her family, he ended it. Applewhite resigned from the university, citing depression and emotional issues. Emotionally unstable and unable to hold a job, he sank into a deep depression following his father's death.

In 1972, Applewhite met nurse Bonnie Nettles, who shared Applewhite's interest in biblical prophecy and theosophy. With so many common interests, the two immediately became close friends. In fact, Applewhite felt as though he had met Nettles in a past life, and Nettles told him that their meeting had been foretold—or previously indicated—to her by aliens, as she persuaded Applewhite that he had a divine assignment.

Applewhite had already begun looking into alternatives to the Christian doctrine, taking up astrology. He even had a vision that he was selected for a similar role to Jesus. Applewhite moved in with Nettles, and despite the relationship being nonsexual, Nettles's husband divorced her, which resulted in Nettles's losing custody of her children.

Because he had broken off communication with his family, Applewhite's world revolved solely around Nettles. The two opened a bookstore together called the Christian Arts Center, as well as a

Marshall Applewhite, leader of the Heaven's Gate cult, believed he would be killed, brought back to life, and transported onto a spaceship.

Bonnie Nettles was a nurse who shared Applewhite's interest in biblical prophecy. The two traveled together, finding new followers for their religion.

teaching facility called Known Place, where they taught classes on mysticism and theosophy. The businesses were unsuccessful and closed shortly after they opened.

In 1973, the pair traveled to the Southwest and western United States to teach people their beliefs. The two converted their first follower in 1974—a friend from Houston who believed and accepted their teachings. Applewhite and Nettles adopted their own religious outline, based on the writings and teachings of various authors, religious teachings, and science fiction works. They believed that they had been chosen to fulfill prophecies in the Bible and were specifically named as the two witnesses cited in the Book of Revelation. Applewhite and Nettles called themselves "The Two," or "The UFO Two," and even believed that they would be killed and then brought back to life and transported onto a spaceship.[4]

After spending six months in jail for not returning a rental car, Applewhite and Nettles sought to contact extraterrestrials and continued building their following, publishing advertisements to recruit disciples, who they referred to as "crew." The cult became known as the "Human Individual Metamorphosis," and they targeted college campuses to recruit followers.

By 1975, the cult had roughly seventy followers and continued mixing beliefs of extraterrestrials, Scientology, and the New Testament, among others. Cult members were told to renounce everything they once knew—family, friends, media, drugs, alcohol, facial hair, jewelry, and sexuality—and to adopt biblical names.

After first living on campgrounds and houses funded by donations from followers, things changed for Applewhite. Nettles passed away in 1985 from complications of a surgery to remove a cancerous tumor from her eye. In the aftermath of Nettles's death, Applewhite became obsessed with the idea that his cult was conspiring against him. Fearing a government raid on the cult's houses, he began to speak more about the Apocalypse. The cult kept a low profile throughout the rest of the 1980s, with followers coming and going, and by the early 1990s, the cult shrank to around twenty-six members. With numbers that low, Applewhite felt a sense of urgency and changed their name to "Total Overcomers Anonymous." He took out a full-page advertisement in *USA Today* that warned about the "catastrophic judgement to befall the Earth."[5] Applewhite was able to double the cult's membership, but it was also at this time that he began to speak more and more about suicide. He renamed the cult "Heaven's Gate."

In 1996, the cult, with its new name, relocated to a mansion in Rancho Santa Fe, California, where they taped two videos that offered viewers a chance to evacuate Earth. Applewhite truly thought that Nettles was in a spaceship and was going to join the cult in the afterlife. The cult began recording farewell statements, as they believed death was near.

Their suicides began in March of 1997, with followers mixing drugs and alcohol and placing bags over their heads. The suicides occurred over a three-day period. Applewhite was one of the last cult members to die. An anonymous tip led the sheriff's department to the cult's mansion. They discovered the bodies, including Applewhite's, which was found in a sitting position on the bed. All in all, thirty-nine dead bodies were found on March 26, and it's now known as the largest group suicide in the United States. While Applewhite didn't commit murder, it was his beliefs and formation of the cult that led to the mass suicide of the members of this religious cult.

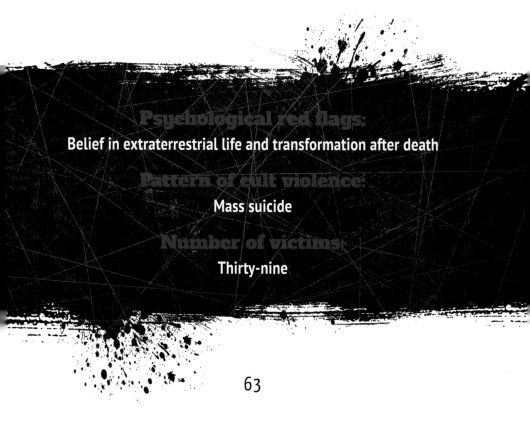

Psychological red flags:

Belief in extraterrestrial life and transformation after death

Pattern of cult violence:

Mass suicide

Number of victims:

Thirty-nine

Prem Kumar
aka "Swami Premananda"

Born: November 17, 1951
Occupation: Spiritual guru
Arrested: 1994 to 1997
Died: February 21, 2011

Prem Kumar was born in 1951 to a merchant family in Matale, Sri Lanka. From a young age, it was evident that he was destined to live a "spiritual life." His parents referred to him as "Ravi," which meant the sun, due to his radiant smile. Others began to take notice, as his spiritual devotion and religious demonstrations became famous. It's said that in October 1969, while the seventeen-year-old was giving a spiritual speech to roughly two hundred people, his clothes began to turn orange—a miracle. From that point forward, Kumar declared that he would dedicate his life to spiritual service, and that he would show God's love to as many people as he could during his lifetime.[6] In 1972, Kumar started his first ashram—or spiritual monastery—that hosted people from all different walks of life, including poor people and homeless children. Kumar toured the world, giving spiritual talks to welcoming listeners in Singapore, Malaysia, the Philippines, and the United Kingdom.

Things changed for Kumar and his ashram in 1983, though, as Sri Lanka was overcome by ethnic riots. Kumar was a prime target of those riots due to his spiritual existence, and his ashram was burned down.

In 1984, Kumar moved to India with his followers, and in 1989, he founded the Sri Premananda Ashram, once again opening the doors to women and orphan children who needed shelter, as well as two hundred other followers. By the end of 1989, the ashram had opened branches in other countries, including the United Kingdom, Switzerland, and Belgium, and he also had founded an international youth wing. It all sounded great, until 1994.

Arul Jyothi, a girl living in the ashram, escaped and reported that she was pregnant and had been raped. Jyothi's testimony prompted a police investigation of the ashram. The investigation uncovered the fact that a follower living in the ashram, Ravi—a different man from Prem Kumar—had been murdered because he planned to expose the devious acts that were occurring inside the cult. Additionally, it was also uncovered at this time that Kumar had raped more than ten girls, including some who were below the age of consent, which was sixteen.

During the trial against Kumar, his lawyer claimed that his client had divine powers and was capable of performing miracles, and also that some of the women in the ashram had consented to the sexual acts, despite the fact that they were under the age of sixteen.

Kumar was ultimately found guilty when samples from Jyothi's fetus confirmed that he was the father, and when the remains of Ravi were found on the ashram's property.

On August 20, 1997, Kumar was sentenced to life in prison for thirteen counts of rape, the molestation of two girls, and the murder of Ravi. Kumar was also fined 67.3 lakhs ($100,000 USD), and his

Prem Kumar was found guilty of murder and sentenced to life in prison

failure to pay the fine carried an additional thirty-two years and nine months of jail time. He received another year of time for cheating the members of his ashram. In addition to Kumar, six of his disciples were found guilty of conspiracy to commit rape and destroying the evidence, with five of them also receiving life sentences. Kumar died in jail on February 21, 2011, due to acute liver failure.

Psychological red flags:

Belief in spiritual miracles and creation of an ashram

Pattern of cult violence:

Rape, molestation

Number of victims:

One

Ervil LeBaron

aka the "Mormon Manson"

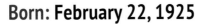

Born: **February 22, 1925**
Occupation: **Religious cult leader**
Arrested: **June 1, 1979**
Died: **August 16, 1981**

Ervil LeBaron, who became known as the "Mormon Manson," was a prominent religious cult leader from the 1970s to the early 1980s. Born into a Mormon family that believed in the practice of polygamy, LeBaron's father, Alma Dayer LeBaron Sr., moved the family to Mexico in 1924 after the LDS—The Church of Jesus Christ of Latter-day Saints—formally abandoned the practice of polygamy. In Mexico, the family started "Colonia LeBaron," a farm where the family could practice and worship the way they wanted to. The leadership of the family and community was handed over to Joel LeBaron, Ervil's older brother, when Alma passed away in 1951. Joel started the community as the "Church of the Firstborn of the Fulness of Times." He moved the community—which numbered around thirty families—and settled in Salt Lake City, Utah, as well as in a community on the Baja California Peninsula called "Los Molinos." Ervil served as his brother's second-in-command in the early years of Joel's reign, but eventually Ervil challenged his brother's leadership and broke away to start his own community, called the "Church of the Lamb of God" in San Diego, California, in 1972.

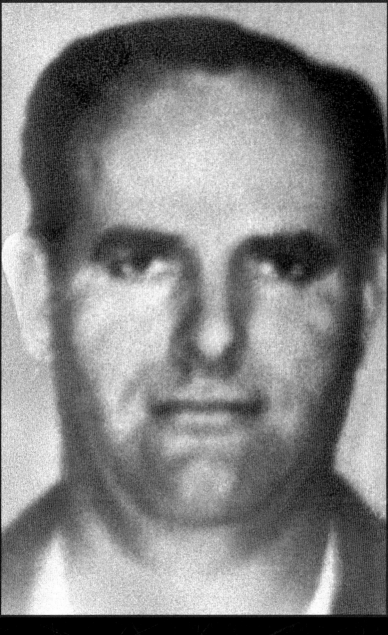

Ervil LeBaron was fifty-four years old in this photo taken in 1977. He was known as the Mormon Manson.

The People Behind Cult Murders

From this point forward, Ervil became obsessed with power, and believed that God started telling him to kill people. First on Ervil's agenda was his brother Joel; Ervil ordered someone to murder Joel in Mexico. Ervil was tried for this murder but the conviction was overturned on a technicality. Many believe this was the direct result of a bribe, which resulted in Ervil getting off scot-free.[7] With Joel dead, Ervil's younger brother, Verlan, took over. Despite Ervil attempting to have his brother Verlan murdered multiple times, the plots were unsuccessful.

Ervil and his cult then focused their attention on rival polygamous leaders. Ervil himself was a polygamist, having at least thirteen wives and fifty children during his life. In April 1975, Ervil arranged the killing of Bob Simons, also a polygamist. In 1977, he authorized the death of Rulon C. Allred, the leader of the "Apostolic United Brethren," a Mormon fundamentalist sect. Ervil's thirteenth wife, Rena Chynoweth, along with another follower, Ramona Marston, committed the murder of Allred. While Chynoweth was tried and found not guilty of the murder, she confessed to the murder in a memoir and also detailed the mind control and fear that Ervil used to control his followers.

Throughout his reign, Ervil took down anyone in his way, or anyone he thought to be standing in his way. Ervil had his family and followers do the dirty work. His tenth wife, Vonda White, was sentenced to life in prison for murdering one of Ervil's followers, Dean Grover Vest. It also wasn't out of the norm for him to have members of his own family killed, including his own seventeen-year-old daughter Rebecca; she was pregnant with her second child and planning to leave the community. When it was all said and done, Ervil was responsible for at least twenty-five murders.

On June 1, 1979, Ervil was caught by the Mexican police, sent back to the United States, and imprisoned for ordering the murder of Allred. In 1980, he was sentenced to life in prison at Utah State Prison, but he died in his cell as a result of myocardial infarction on August 16, 1981. Prior to his death and while in prison, Ervil wrote a four-hundred-page "bible" entitled *The Book of the New Covenants*. This book called for the killings of disobedient church members and contained a hit list of his top targets. Several of his disciples followed his word, killing four people, including an eight-year-old girl, at 4:00 p.m. on June 27, 1988, in what are now known as the "4 O'Clock Murders." Following those killings, five cult members were found guilty of murder, including Ervil's daughter, Jacqueline LeBaron, who spent seventeen years on the run from the police before being extradited to the United States from Honduras.

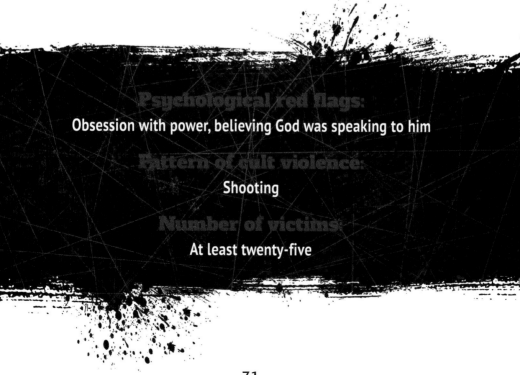

Psychological red flags:

Obsession with power, believing God was speaking to him

Pattern of cult violence:

Shooting

Number of victims:

At least twenty-five

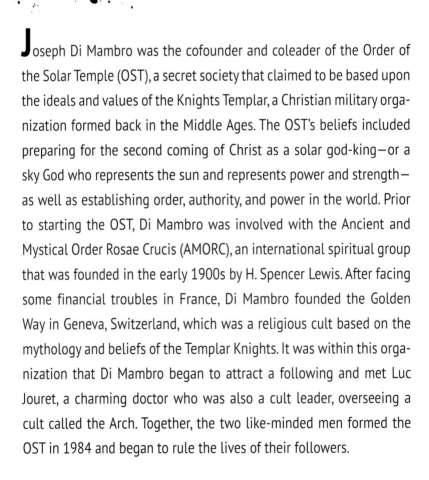

Born: August 19, 1924
Occupation: Religious figure
Died: October 5, 1994

Joseph Di Mambro was the cofounder and coleader of the Order of the Solar Temple (OST), a secret society that claimed to be based upon the ideals and values of the Knights Templar, a Christian military organization formed back in the Middle Ages. The OST's beliefs included preparing for the second coming of Christ as a solar god-king—or a sky God who represents the sun and represents power and strength— as well as establishing order, authority, and power in the world. Prior to starting the OST, Di Mambro was involved with the Ancient and Mystical Order Rosae Crucis (AMORC), an international spiritual group that was founded in the early 1900s by H. Spencer Lewis. After facing some financial troubles in France, Di Mambro founded the Golden Way in Geneva, Switzerland, which was a religious cult based on the mythology and beliefs of the Templar Knights. It was within this organization that Di Mambro began to attract a following and met Luc Jouret, a charming doctor who was also a cult leader, overseeing a cult called the Arch. Together, the two like-minded men formed the OST in 1984 and began to rule the lives of their followers.

The two men each had separate roles within the cult, with Jouret giving lectures to attract new members and Di Mambro running the cult and managing its finances. He claimed that he was operating under the direction of "masters," whom no one ever saw. It's been said that Di Mambro's control over his followers was so strong that he would decide when they could have children and what the children's names would be.[8] After moving the cult to Quebec, Canada, in the mid-1980s, the OST tacked onto their beliefs, adding astrology, medieval legends, and even Christianity. At the height of its time, the cult was comprised of more than four hundred followers. Aside from the force that the two leaders had over their cult, they were also charging their followers for being members, and that allowed Di Mambro to buy real estate around the world in countries like Australia, France, Switzerland, and Canada. Jouret and Di Mambro continued to fill their followers' heads with unrealistic ideas and beliefs, with Di Mambro even going as far as to say that his son Elie was created by theogamy—or marriage of the gods—and that his daughter Emmanuelle was conceived without sexual intercourse.

Things began to deteriorate for the OST in 1991. Di Mambro was being doubted by his followers and even his own son. The cult's activities came under investigation by the Canadian authorities. As a direct result, Jouret and Di Mambro moved the cult to Switzerland to escape investigation. They stayed in Switzerland for a few years, but by 1994, the cult came to an abrupt end. Di Mambro and Jouret believed in the transformative powers of fire and thought they could be reborn on Sirius, a different planet in another universe. They set fire to the cult's buildings, killing at least forty-eight people, including Jouret and Di Mambro, his wife, and his children.

Officials search what remains of one of the buildings of the Order of the Solar Temple in Montreal, Canada.

At the scene of the crime, investigators also found bodies that had been injected with tranquilizers or had plastic bags over their heads, as well as followers who had been shot, leading to the belief that some people were murdered while others committed suicide. Some of the bodies were dressed in OST robes and found lying in a circle inside a secret underground chapel. Others—bodies of children—were found lying in a ski chalet. Authorities concluded that many of the victims were drugged prior to being shot. Additionally, a couple with an infant son had been murdered prior to the fires, with reports that Di Mambro ordered the killing of the family because he believed that the boy was the Antichrist. The infant was stabbed repeatedly with a wooden stake, as Di Mambro believed the Antichrist was born to prevent him from succeeding in his spiritual calling. The death of Di Mambro left a lot of unanswered questions regarding the cult and its activities, but it was uncovered that some cult followers had donated more than C$1 million ($715,461 USD) to Di Mambro.

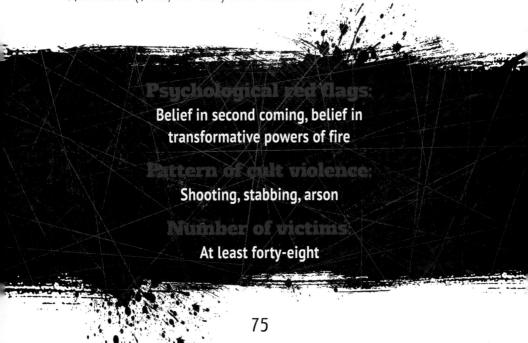

Psychological red flags:

Belief in second coming, belief in transformative powers of fire

Pattern of cult violence:

Shooting, stabbing, arson

Number of victims:

At least forty-eight

Chapter 4

The Murderous Leaders and Followers of

DOOMSDAY CULTS

It's not one of the more well-known types of cults to the average person, but doomsday cults date back to the days of the Pilgrims. Led usually by ministers or preachers, these groups recruit individuals and convince these members to cut off all ties and communication to the outside world, including with their family members. These cults have a set of guidelines and rules that they live by, which are created and managed by the leader. And while the leader creates the rules, the leader is not governed by the same rules because he or she is seen as being directly connected to God or another superior being. The claim of being connected to a higher being causes many of the cult members to worship the leader as if he or she is God—this is where doomsday cults can be seen as very similar to a lot of other types of cults. With the help of the leader, the doomsday cult members believe that they are a chosen group of people who have been selected to be saved from the end of the world. These beliefs are loosely based on the Bible or other religious doctrines. All in all, "doomsday" is usually seen as the end of the universe.

Doomsday cults are usually formed by a charismatic leader who recruits individuals with a number of techniques. One of the most common ways is to invite them to a nonthreatening event. These types of events could range from a party, concert, or spiritual reading. Once there, the leader uses a technique called "love-bombing" to recruit members. Love-bombing involves praising and showing attention to potential members, which causes them to feel good about themselves as well as the leader. As the love-bombing continues, the individual begins to trust the leader.

Once the leader has gained the attention of the follower, he or she reveals a "prize" to the individual. This "prize" could be helping others or learning one's purpose in life, which is nothing more than an ulterior motive for the better good of the cult. In the end, the recruit finds the offer appealing and thus becomes a member of the cult.

The members of a doomsday cult are forbidden from having contact with individuals on the "outside" and are isolated from the real world. This isolation not only includes the people but also the technologies that are present in the world. For example, these individuals are not allowed to have cellular phones, computers, or any devices that can connect them to the life that they left behind. Of course, rules can vary across different types and different leaders of doomsday cults, but these are the most common rules noted.

The group leader manipulates the cult members by using certain mind control tactics. These tactics often include isolation and

Members of doomsday cults believe that they have been selected to be saved from the end of the world.

separation from the outside world. The leader also utilizes certain methods that can deter the thought processes of the doomsday cult members. These methods include mandatory meditation from the members, repetitious activities, and even chanting. The leaders of these groups also use sleep deprivation, fear, guilt, and insufficient nutrition in order to control members and keep them from leaving the group.

aka "The Prophet"

Born: **1932**

Occupation: **Cult leader**

Diagnosis: **Bipolar disorder**

Died: **Confirmation of death is unknown**

While Joseph Kibweteere was a religious man, his cult most certainly falls into the doomsday category. He was born in Uganda and raised as a Roman Catholic. He was wealthy by Ugandan standards; in 1980, he ran for political office and had enough land to donate for a Catholic school that he was designing. He opened the school and was seen as a positive figure within the community. During this time, Uganda was under heavy religious and political upheaval, which influenced Kibweteere. At this time in Uganda, Idi Amin's rule, the acquired immunodeficiency syndrome (AIDS) epidemic, and the Ugandan Bush War created chaos throughout the country. Kibweteere used religion as an escape from the chaos; some of his stronger religious beliefs at this time included beliefs in miracles and Marian apparitions, or the belief in a supernatural appearance by the Blessed Virgin Mary. In fact, Kibweteere claimed to have experienced a sighting of the Virgin Mary in 1984.

Fast-forward to 1989, when Kibweteere (a married man) met Credonia Mwerinde, a prostitute who was looking to repent for her sins. Mwerinde also had claimed to have seen the Virgin Mary when looking at a stone in the mountains, and with their joint beliefs the two formed the doomsday cult, the "Movement of the Restoration of the Ten Commandments of God." While the roots of the cult can be traced back to Mwerinde's father, Paul Kashaku, Kibweteere became the official leader after Kashaku's death.

The mission of the cult was to obey the Ten Commandments and preach the word of Jesus Christ. One of the underlying messages was that in order to avoid the damnation of the Apocalypse, they had to strictly follow and obey the Commandments. This message was both enforced and accepted by the cult so much that the members were discouraged from even speaking, for fear of breaking the Ninth Commandment, "Thou shalt not bear false witness against thy neighbor." Inside the cult, fasts were conducted regularly, with only one meal eaten on Fridays and Mondays. Both sex and soap were forbidden.

As the leader of the group, Kibweteere emphasized apocalypticism—or the belief that the world will soon come to an end—and with Mwerinde's help, the two authored a booklet, *A Timely Message from Heaven: The End of the Present Time*. Kibweteere stated several dates on the calendar in which the world would end, which came and went uneventfully. Kibweteere did state though that the year 2000 would be followed by "year 1 of the new world," which would foreshadow what was to come. The arrival of Dominic Kataribabo, a popular priest, to the cult helped to grow the acclaim of the cult. By selling land that he owned, Kibweteere built up the cult, building houses and primary schools.

By 1997, the Movement listed itself as having close to five thousand members, and despite being shut down in 1998 for unsanitary conditions, the use of child labor, and kidnapping children,

The People Behind Cult Murders

Ugandan policemen put up a sign telling people to keep out of the church grounds of the Restoration of the Ten Commandments of God cult in southwest Uganda. The remains of up to four hundred doomsday cult members who died were buried in a common grave.

the cult was allowed to reopen. In 2000, it began to prepare for the end of the world by slaughtering cattle and buying large amounts of Coca-Cola for their feast. But when January 1, 2000, came and went without the world ending, cult members began questioning their leader's beliefs, and the movement began to unravel. To combat the pushback from his members, Kibweteere proclaimed that March 17, 2000, would be the new end of the world, which he orchestrated for his members. On March 17, 530 members were killed when a fire roared through their church during a service; authorities found that the windows and doors of the church had been boarded up. Kibweteere himself is speculated to have been killed in the fire, although there are conflicting theories that Kibweteere and other cult officials fled and are still alive.[1]

While investigating the church fire, authorities located hundreds more dead bodies of past cult members at various sites in southern Uganda, and the total death toll was settled at 778. It was ruled that the additional bodies that were found were murdered weeks before the church fire, mostly using poison, with all signs pointing to Kibweteere and other high-ranking officials orchestrating the mass murder.

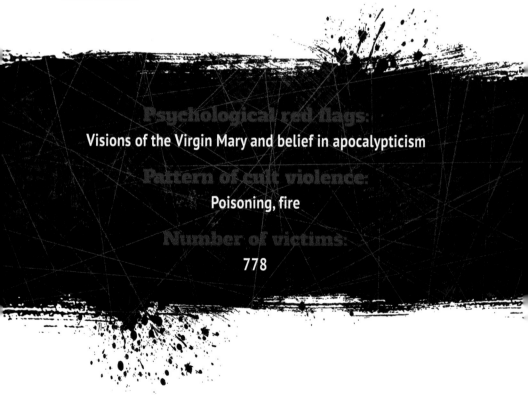

Psychological red flags:

Visions of the Virgin Mary and belief in apocalypticism

Pattern of cult violence:

Poisoning, fire

Number of victims:

778

Shoko Asahara

Born: **March 2, 1955**

Occupation: **Pharmacist/cult leader**

Arrested: **May 16, 1995**

On March 20, 1995, twelve commuters in Tokyo were killed when nerve gas was released on the subway at the hands of "Aum Shinrikyo," a doomsday cult led by Shoko Asahara. Born Chizuo Matsumoto, Asahara was born half blind to a poor Japanese family in 1955. He was the only partially sighted student at a school for the blind.[2] After graduating from school in 1977, Asahara got married in 1978. He started selling herbal mixtures and performing acupuncture, but got into trouble because he was practicing without a pharmaceutical license. He was fined 200,000 yen ($1,651 USD). Then he shifted his efforts toward starting a religious movement. In 1987 Asahara changed his name and applied for government registration for a cult he was creating, called Aum Shinrikyo, or "religion of truth." The cult's religion was a blend of Hindu and Buddhist spirituality that also included the teachings of the Bible's Revelations and the writings of Nostradamus. Shortly after the cult was approved, he established a monastic order for the group, which led to an increase in followers. He began building up his name, appearing on television and in magazines, and speaking at public lectures. This exposure led to an increase in cult membership.

Shoko Asahara was the guru of doomsday cult Aum Shinrikyo.

The People Behind Cult Murders

Asahara's cult was based on the beliefs that the world was destined for destruction, and that he was the savior who would lead the spiritually pure to salvation. At the height of the cult's success, it's said that there were more than ten thousand members in Aum Shinrikyo, spanning across Japan and additional countries, like Russia. Make no mistake about it, though—Asahara was a brutal cult leader. Meals for his followers didn't come often, and members were allowed to sleep for only about three hours each day. Perhaps the most bizarre and controlling aspect was that most members were forced to wear helmets that contained electrodes attached to their scalps, which sent small electric shocks between them and their leader. Asahara believed that his followers could only truly connect with him and his beliefs when their brain waves were connected with his. To fund the helmets and the rest of the cult's operation, members were required to donate all of their money and wealth to the cult, and members were even charged extra for things like books, initiation ceremonies, and the helmets. Inside of the cult's compounds, Asahara had brilliant scientists working on diabolical biological weapons that attack the body's nervous system, causing major organs to shut down one by one until the heart gives up. Along these lines, it's been said that Asahara admired Hitler, who used similar methods to kill.[3]

Asahara and his cult used those deadly gases in the Tokyo subway attack on March 20, 1995. Up to twelve people died, and thousands of people were rushed to the hospital to be treated for inhalation of the deadly gas. Following the subway attack, police linked Asahara and Aum Shinrikyo to the attack as well as to other smaller incidents that had happened just prior to this event. The cult's compound was raided on May 16, 1995, and multiple cult

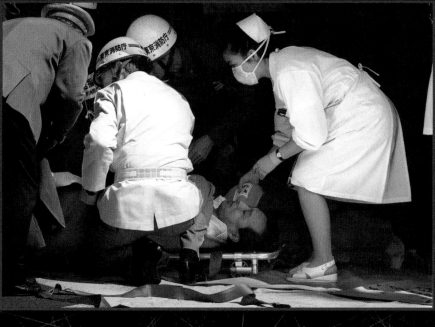

A commuter is treated by an emergency medical team at a shelter after inhaling a lethal nerve gas that was unleashed by the Aum Shinrikyo cult.

members including Asahara were arrested. Around this time, it was also learned that the cult had bigger plans, including attempts to purchase automatic weapons and ammunition, tanks, and even a MiG-29 fighter plane. In court, Asahara was up against twenty-seven murder counts in thirteen separate indictments—including accusations that he directed the Sakamoto family murder. Cult members testified against their leader, and Asahara was found guilty on thirteen of the seventeen charges. He was condemned to death by hanging on February 27, 2004. The sentence has yet to be carried out due to multiple appeals and additional arrests of his cult members.

Psychological red flags:

Belief in the end of the world

Pattern of cult violence:

Poison

Number of victims:

Eleven to twelve

David Koresh

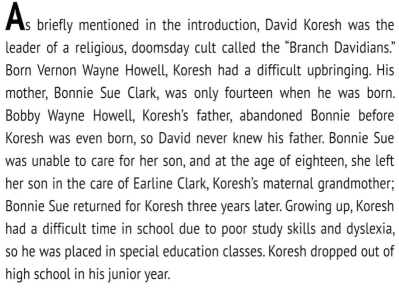

Born: **August 17, 1959**

Occupation: **Musician and cult leader**

Died: **April 19, 1993**

As briefly mentioned in the introduction, David Koresh was the leader of a religious, doomsday cult called the "Branch Davidians." Born Vernon Wayne Howell, Koresh had a difficult upbringing. His mother, Bonnie Sue Clark, was only fourteen when he was born. Bobby Wayne Howell, Koresh's father, abandoned Bonnie before Koresh was even born, so David never knew his father. Bonnie Sue was unable to care for her son, and at the age of eighteen, she left her son in the care of Earline Clark, Koresh's maternal grandmother; Bonnie Sue returned for Koresh three years later. Growing up, Koresh had a difficult time in school due to poor study skills and dyslexia, so he was placed in special education classes. Koresh dropped out of high school in his junior year.

Around the age of twenty-two, Koresh joined his mother's church, the Seventh-day Adventist Church. He was eventually expelled for pursuing the pastor's daughter, after a Bible verse led him to believe that God wanted him to have the pastor's daughter for a wife.

In 1982, Koresh moved to Waco, Texas, and joined the Branch Davidians at the Mount Carmel Center. A spin-off from the

This 1998 photo shows Branch Davidian leader David Koresh in a
police lineup following a gun battle with former Davidians.

Seventh-day Adventist Church, the religious cult was a good fit for Koresh because he was already familiar with the teachings. The cult was led by Ben Roden and his wife, Lois, who had been original members of the Davidian Seventh-day Adventist group but formed their own sect after leader Victor Houteff died. One of the Branch Davidians' strongest movements was that they believed themselves to be living in a time when Bible prophecies of a final divine judgment were coming to pass as a prelude to Christ's Second Coming. Koresh played guitar and sang at church services, and even formed his own band, recruiting members to the cult through music. Around 1983, Koresh began claiming that he was a prophet. It is said that he had a sexual relationship with Lois Roden, after which time Roden allowed Koresh to teach his own message, called "The Serpent's Root."[4] This caused controversy among the other cult members. This especially didn't sit well with Roden's son, George, who believed that he was the cult's next leader. George, with the support of most of the other members, forced Koresh and his group of followers off of the property with guns.

Now on his own with his own group of followers, Koresh moved to Palestine, Texas, where the cult members lived in buses and tents due to low income and support. He began recruiting more followers to his cult, pulling people from California, the United Kingdom, Israel, and Australia. Koresh now had the support of the followers who moved with him to Palestine. At the end of 1987, support for George Roden was declining. Roden challenged Koresh to a contest to see who could raise the dead. Roden went as far as digging up a corpse to demonstrate his spiritual powers. Koresh saw this as an opportunity to get Roden out of the way and have him arrested for illegally exhuming a dead body. The police told Koresh he needed proof though, and when he returned to the Mount Carmel Center along with seven followers armed with guns to get photographic proof, a gun battle broke out and Roden was wounded. Koresh and his followers were arrested for attempted murder. They were acquitted, and coincidentally two years later, Roden was convicted of murder after he murdered Wayman Dale Adair by hitting him in the skull with an axe.

With Roden now locked up, Koresh and his followers took back the Mount Carmel Center. It was also around this time that Koresh, still Vernon Howell at the time, formally changed his name to David Koresh. The last name *Koresh* was chosen because it was the Persian name of Cyrus the Great, a Persian king who was deemed a Messiah for releasing the Jews during the Babylonian Captivity. The first name *David* was chosen for King David. By taking this name, Koresh was affirming himself to be the spiritual offspring of King David.

The fate of the Branch Davidians changed around 1992 when allegations of child abuse and statutory rape began to surface about the cult. Koresh was known to have sexual relations with multiple female followers, including thirteen-year-old Michelle Jones, Koresh's sister-in-law. Koresh had also been described as determined, hardened, manipulative, and paranoid.[5] While a six-month investigation into these allegations didn't lead to any evidence against Koresh, the Bureau of Alcohol, Tobacco and Firearms (ATF), stormed the Mount Carmel Center on February 28, 1993. Four members of the ATF and six cult members were killed during the raid. A fifty-one-day standoff between the Branch Davidians and the FBI's Hostage Rescue Team (HRT) followed, with contact taking place via telephone. The standoff concluded on April 19, when FBI officials were instructed to remove the Branch

The Branch Davidian compound's observation tower is engulfed in flames after a fire started inside. After a shootout that killed four federal agents and six members of the Branch Davidian religious cult,

Davidians by force. In a manner that is still disputed to this day, the church in which Koresh and seventy-nine Branch Davidians—twenty-two of them under the age of seventeen—were barricaded caught fire, and they were killed.[6] The FBI later discovered that Koresh's right-hand man realized they were going to die and shot and killed Koresh before turning the gun on himself.

Psychological red flags:

Claiming gift of prophecy

Pattern of cult violence:

Shooting

Number of victims:

Eighty-four

Chapter 5

The Murderous Leaders and Followers of

POLITICAL AND TERRORIST CULTS

Political and terrorist cults are outside organizations that perform brainwashing and secret initiations to recruit new members. These types of groups recruit people based upon a person's appearance, gender, race, ethnicity, religion, or for other unknown reasons. They prey on people who are desperately in need of change. This is the same reason that gang violence exists in most major cities; people are easily pulled into these sorts of debilitating organizations when they are in a weakened state, and the other opportunities in their environment don't seem realistic.[1]

The political or terrorist cult is typically formed when there is a perceived need for change in a certain region. Though some of the ideals associated with such extremists are often encouraged by the values of society, the cult will nearly always have an alternative agenda that does not consider the happiness, life, and overall well-being of humanity. Cults take advantage of people who need assistance financially or socially. This is true of all cults, but especially true of political cults. Political cults are often backed by an agenda that relates to current politics in a region, and they are often an attempt to overthrow the current political system. Terrorist cults function in a violent manner that is counterproductive to the growth of humanity, and they do this by pursuing destruction of cities and people for idealistic reasons that are sometimes related to religious doctrines. These religious doctrines that fuel terrorism are often taken out of context to better suit the cult's agenda.

The cults that operate on political or terror motivation are often formed by people who are idealistic in their pursuits and often not in grievance with the current state of the world, the state of their country, or the appreciation of their doctrines. The ideals that fuel a terrorist group or political cult do not, however, have to be involved in religious doctrines. These political cults often spring up in societies that are struggling for normalcy. They impact the people who live in the cults' region in a big way. People are recruited into cults based on their demographics, and they are often brainwashed to believe that the cult's agenda is the best available response to society. These extremist groups function on fear and should be approached with extreme caution.

Terrorist cults use violence and threats to intimidate and spread fear.

Osama bin Laden

Born: **March 10, 1957**

Occupation: **Military/terrorist
leader**

Died: **May 2, 2011**

Osama bin Laden's name will forever live in infamy because of his role in the September 11, 2001, attacks on the World Trade Center in New York City. Osama bin Mohammed bin Awad bin Laden, the founder and leader of al-Qaeda, was born in Saudi Arabia in 1957 into a rich family. After his father was killed in a helicopter crash in 1969, bin Laden is believed to have inherited $80 million.[2] Raised as a devout Sunni Muslim, bin Laden's early childhood and upbringing was spent interpreting the Qur'an and jihad (holy Islamic war) for his religion while also attending King Abdulaziz University, where he studied business administration and economics. In 1984, bin Laden traveled to Afghanistan, reportedly responding to calls for a jihad against the Soviets. He took control of twenty thousand Islamic fighters who were recruited from around the world. Along with the help of Abdullah Azzam, bin Laden formed the Maktab al-Khidamat, also known as the Afghan Services Bureau, which aimed to raise funds and recruit soldiers to fight against the Soviets in Afghanistan. For his efforts, bin Laden was revered among fellow Arabs.

In 1988, wanting more of a military role, bin Laden left the Marktab al-Khidamat and formed al-Qaeda, which had membership

Osama bin Laden was the leader of Al Qaeda, a terrorist network responsible for thousands of deaths, including the victims of the attacks on September 11, 2001.

requirements that included having listening ability, good manners, obedience, and making a pledge to follow one's superiors. Believing that the Islamic world was in a crisis, al-Qaeda aimed to "set things right" in bin Laden's eyes. The base ideology of bin Laden and al-Qaeda was that civilians from enemy countries were legitimate targets for jihadists to kill, and that included women and children. Bin Laden also believed that the foreign policy of the United States persecuted, killed, and harmed Muslims in the Middle East, and he opposed secular government, socialism, communism, and

The World Trade Center Complex in New York City still smolders on September 26, 2001, two weeks after terrorists attacked the Twin Towers with hijacked jetliners.

democracy. He was also anti-Semitic and believed most negative events that happened in the world were because of Jewish actions. At the height of his power, bin Laden called for elimination of the Israeli state, instructing the United States to withdraw all of its civilians and military personnel from the Middle East. He was labeled a terrorist by the media as well as government officials.

From 1988 to 2000, al-Qaeda built itself up under bin Laden's control and leadership, training his army and making them believe that they were fighting for the greater good of the Islamic state. Throughout this time, the militant group was tied to several terrorist acts, including but not limited to: the 1993 attack on the World Trade Center in New York in which six people were killed and roughly one thousand were injured; a 1995 bombing of US military advisors to the Saudi national guard that killed five US soldiers and injured more than sixty people; a 1996 bombing at a US military base in Saudi Arabia that killed nineteen US nationals and wounded 386 more; multiple 1998 bomb attacks against US embassies in Nairobi and Dar-es-Salaam that killed 224 people and left thousands more injured; and a 2000 suicide attack in the port of Aden in Yemen that killed seventeen US Marines and wounded thirty-eight more.[3] Libya issued an Interpol arrest warrant on March 16, 1998, for bin Laden for the killing of German domestic intelligence service agent, Silvan Becker, and his wife, Vera. He was also indicted by a US Federal Grand Jury for his participation in the 1998 US embassy bombings in Nairobi and Dar-es-Salaam. In June 1999, he became the 456th criminal listed on the FBI's Ten Most Wanted Fugitives list.

Then came the day that lives in US infamy—September 11, 2011—when bin Laden orchestrated al-Qaeda's hijacking of four US airplanes, crashing them into the two towers of New York's World

Osama bin Laden was killed in his compound in Abbottabad, Pakistan, by US special forces.

Trade Center, the Pentagon near Washington, DC, and a field in rural Pennsylvania. This terrorist act killed at least three thousand people and left the entire nation saddened, hardened, and distraught, while bin Laden hid in the Middle East.

Following the attacks, the United States declared a War on Terror while also placing a $25 million bounty on bin Laden. For the next ten years, the US military led an endless hunt for bin Laden. That hunt eventually came to an end on May 2, 2011, when SEAL (sea, air, land) Team Six raided bin Laden's compound in Abbottabad, Pakistan, killing him in the process.

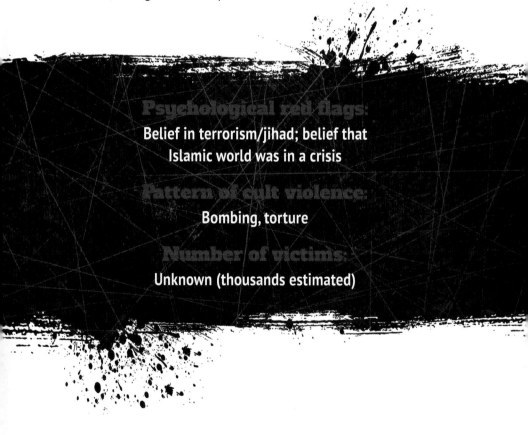

Psychological red flags:

Belief in terrorism/jihad; belief that Islamic world was in a crisis

Pattern of cult violence:

Bombing, torture

Number of victims:

Unknown (thousands estimated)

Abimael Guzmán
aka "President Gonzalo"

> **Born: December 3, 1934**
> **Occupation: Philosophy professor**
> **Arrested: September 12, 1992**

Born in Peru, Guzmán had a difficult upbringing. To start, he was the illegitimate son of a man who had won the nation's lottery and had six children with three different women. Guzmán's mother, Berenice, passed away when he was five, and for the next seven years, Guzmán lived with his mother's family. At the age of nineteen, he enrolled at the San Agustin National University as a student in the social studies department. He became attracted to Marxism, as he was heavily influenced by Jose Carlos Mariategui's *Seven Essays on the Interpretation of the Peruvian Reality*. Mariategui was the founder of the Communist Party in Peru.

After completing bachelor's degrees in philosophy and law, he was recruited by San Cristobal of Huamanga University as a professor of philosophy. The man who recruited him, Dr. Efrain Morote Best, eventually became the philosophical leader of the "Shining Path movement," a cult that Guzmán would lead. While recruiting Guzmán, Dr. Best also attracted several other like-minded individuals in an attempt to start a revolution in Peru.

It was around this time that the Peruvian Community Party fractured over ideological and personal disputes, leading to

Guzmán's emergence as the leader of the Shining Path. The Shining Path is a Maoist guerilla insurgent system that heavily bases its belief and formation around Marxism-Leninism, which is described by the *New World Encyclopedia* as, "the belief that a revolutionary proletarian class would not emerge automatically from capitalism. Instead, there was the need for a professional revolutionary party to lead the working class in the violent overthrow of capitalism, to be followed by a dictatorship of the proletariat as the first stage toward communism."[4] Guzmán adopted the nickname "Presidente Gonzalo" and started to preach for a peasant-led revolution. His followers declared him to be the "Fourth Sword of Communism" following Karl Marx, Vladimir Lenin, and Mao Zedong.

During the late 1970s, the Shining Path cult movement grew larger than just academic circles in Peruvian universities. It spread into a guerilla group within Ayacucho, the city capital of the Huamanga Province in the Ayacucho Region of Peru. In 1980, the cult started a war against the Peruvian government, burning ballot boxes in a village near Ayacucho in an effort to hinder the democratic elections. The group's overall purpose was to disrupt and undermine the Peruvian government, and they did just that, launching more attacks as they gained control of central and southern Peru and sections of Lima. Government employees at all levels were targeted by the Shining Path, including the army, police, and other government officials and employees as well as any peasants or middle-class people who cooperated with the government. It's been estimated by the Truth and Reconciliation Commission that nearly seventy thousand people lost their lives in this conflict, mostly through bombings and other vicious acts. At least half of these deaths were sanctioned by the Shining Path.[5]

Abimael Guzmán is spending life in prison for terrorism and murder.

Additionally, the cult began to receive a negative reputation in the area due to their public punishment of corrupt government officials. Because of this, strict curfews were enforced, alcohol was prohibited, fear heightened, and people began to switch sides and rally for the military instead of the Shining Path. This led to even more violence in the area, with the Shining Path murdering sixty-nine people, including women and children. This 1983 event is now known as the Lucanamarca Massacre.

With every violent act that Guzmán and his cult committed, his personal image as an unemotional murderer grew larger. Guzmán started to believe that the Shining Path had escalated from waging a war for the people to waging a war of movements, taking a step toward achieving strategic equilibrium.

In 1992, however, Guzmán and his murderous cult were hit hard by authorities. Authorities believed the terrorist cult members of the Shining Path were using residences within Lima as safe houses. On September 12, 1992, authorities raided a dance studio and found Guzman located on the second floor. They arrested him along with eight other cult members. During the raid, authorities seized Guzmán's computer, which contained information on his entire regime, including its weapons, soldiers, and support base within each region of the country. Some of the details included the Shining Path having 23,430 members along with 235 revolvers, 500 rifles, and 300 other military hardware items, such as grenades.

At the trial, military judges wore hoods because the Shining Path was known for targeting judges who put their cult members in prison. The trial took only three days, and Guzmán was sentenced to life in prison. In 2003, more than five thousand people appealed the ruling, and a retrial was awarded when the court declared that the military trials were unconstitutional. Again, Guzmán was incarcerated for life on charges of aggravated terrorism and murder, and he is currently serving the life sentence in a maximum security prison at Callao, a naval base in Peru.[6]

Psychological red flags:

Belief in Marxism-Leninism; leading of revolution against government

Pattern of cult violence:

Bombing, torture

Number of victims:

Unknown (thousands estimated)

Abu Musab al-Zarqawi
aka "Shaykh of the Slaughterers"

Born: **October 30, 1966**

Occupation: **Military/terrorist leader**

Died: **June 7, 2006**

Abu Musab al-Zarqawi, who was born in Jordan as Ahmad Fadeel al-Nazal al-Khalayleh, was a militant Islamist. He's most known for being the leader of al-Qaeda from 2004 to 2006, orchestrating a series of bombings, beheadings, and attacks in what's known to some as a Shia–Sunni civil war. Not much is known about Zarqawi's childhood other than the fact that he was a high school dropout and a petty criminal. Zarqawi briefly met Osama bin Laden in the late 1980s when Zarqawi was working in Afghanistan as a reporter for an Islamic newsletter. Zarqawi returned to Jordan between 1989 and 1992 to help start Jund al-Sham, a local militant terrorist group. In 1992, Zarqawi was arrested and imprisoned after weapons, including guns and explosives, were found inside his home. In prison, he was known as one of the toughest prisoners in his cellblock, and adopted further radical Islamic beliefs, which became evident when he was released from prison.

Zarqawi was released in 1999 and immediately forced to flee to Pakistan when his involvement in the millennium plot—the plan to bomb the Jordanian Radisson SAS Hotel prior to New Year's Day in 2000—was spoiled. When Zarqawi's Pakistan visa was revoked, he went to Afghanistan and met with Osama bin Laden and additional Al Qaeda leaders. They gave Zarqawi the permission and funds ($200,000 USD) to start his own militant training camp, called Jama'at al-Tawhid wal-Jihad. The camp attracted many Jordanian militants.[7]

In October 2001, Zarqawi was in Afghanistan fighting alongside the Taliban and Al Qaeda. He suffered cracked ribs and fled to Iran to receive medical treatment. Over the course of the next two years, Zarqawi's whereabouts weren't concrete; some believe he was training a group of militants in Syria while other intelligence agencies believe he was in Baghdad until late 2002. During this time, Zarqawi appeared on the US list of most-wanted al-Qaeda terrorists yet to be apprehended.

Fast-forward to 2003. Zarqawi had started to build up his own terror network, setting up sleeper cells and military resistance units in Iraq and Iran to oppose the involvement of the United States in the War on Terror.[8] Over the next three years, Zarqawi and his terrorist group, Jama'at al-Tawhid wal-Jihad, were accused of more than a dozen violent and deadly terrorist attacks in Iraq. Zarqawi took credit for some. Among his targets were many high-ranking officials and government buildings as well as civilians and Christian churches. Zarqawi targeted anyone he felt was oppressing or humiliating the Islamic people or the Islamic nation. October 2004 saw Zarqawi formally pledge loyalty to bin Laden and alter the name of his terrorist group to Tanẓ'īm Qā'idat al-Jihād fī Bilād al-Rāfidayn, which became known as al-Qaeda in Iraq.[9] Zarqawi gave al-Qaeda an unmistakable presence at a time when most of its leaders were killed or in hiding as a result of the September 11, 2001, terrorist attacks. He used his media knowledge to broadcast attacks and

Abu Musab al-Zarqawi speaks on television in 2006.

beheadings to shed light on the power of al-Qaeda. It's important to note that bin Laden and other al-Qaeda leaders didn't always agree with Zarqawi's methods of independent attacks and his anti-Shia stance.

Between 2004 and 2006, the United States, under President George W. Bush, heavily tracked Zarqawi. On October 15, 2004, the US State Department put him and his militant group on its list of foreign terrorist organizations and put a stop on any of the group's assets that may have existed within the United States. By May 2005, Zarqawi was the most wanted man in Iraq and Jordan due to his violent terrorist attacks; the US government proposed a

$25 million reward for any clues that could lead to Zarqawi's apprehension. On June 7, 2006, Zarqawi was killed in a targeted attack while at a meeting in an isolated safe house in Iraq. Two five hundred-pound laser-guided bombs were dropped over the house by the US Air Force, and five others were also killed. US officials had been tracking Zarqawi and were able to confirm his location with the help of Jordanian intelligence officials.

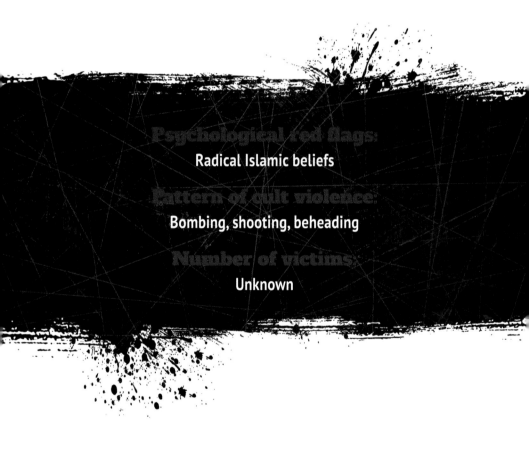

Psychological red flags:

Radical Islamic beliefs

Pattern of cult violence:

Bombing, shooting, beheading

Number of victims:

Unknown

CONCLUSION

While there's no exact science or genetic makeup as to what drives a person to become a murderous cult leader, it's clear to see that there are behaviors and personalities that make up these types of individuals. From a personality like Charles Manson—who had an unstable childhood and early criminal history—to someone like Osama bin Laden—who was born into money but sought to follow his religious beliefs—these murderers come from all different walks of life. Yet, all of these individuals have similar traits, including strong beliefs, the need to be in control, a lack of remorse or guilt, an obsession with power, and complete disregard for the law, among many other things. It's often been wondered if these types of individuals can be rehabilitated; in the case of the cult leaders named in this text, many of them don't get that opportunity because they're killed before ever being caught by the authorities.

The People Behind Cult Murders

Dr. Paul Mountjoy, who spoke to Charles Manson multiple times while he was incarcerated, believes that their environment plays a large contributing factor in their behavior, saying, "Sociopaths often also suffer from narcissistic personality disorder, making it extremely difficult to treat them with any measure of success. Narcissists make it even more difficult for mental health care professionals to weed through their exploitive behaviors. Genetics play a strong role in the disorder, but it is also heavily influenced by environmental factors. As children, those with ASPD (Antisocial Personality Disorder) often demonstrate anger, defiance, screaming, violence, and outward hate of anything normal."[1]

For those who have been victimized by a cult or cult leader, there are organizations and medical facilities that can help with rehabilitation and acclimatization back to everyday life. CultHelp. info and FreedomOfMind.com offer services that include helping individuals come out of a cult. Many psychologists also specialize in this practice area, receiving training in symptoms like post-traumatic stress disorder (PTSD) and depression, as well as learning how to reintegrate their patients back into society. A simple Google search for psychologists in your area or a call to your health insurance company can help you identify practicing psychologists in your area. *Psychology Today*'s website can also serve as an excellent resource for information on cult recovery and location of psychologists and therapists based in your state. Although it can be difficult to break the physical, psychological, emotional, and spiritual ties to that cult or leader, it can indeed be done with the help of a licensed professional or organization. David Ayliffe, who was a member of the "Zion Full Salvation Ministry" and had his finances, family rela-tionships, and dignity stripped by the cult, was able to overcome the mental and emotional damage he suffered via the cult by seeking professional help and joining a support group. You can read more about David's story in his book, *My Brother's Eyes*.[2] For those who have never been affected by a cult, it's important that we continue to support and remember those who have been hurt or who have lost loved ones at the hands of a cult or group. One example is the National September 11 Memorial & Museum in New York.

Chapter Notes

Introduction

1. Mark Roth, "Experts Track the Patterns of Mass Murders," *Pittsburgh Post-Gazette,* April 13, 2009, http://www.post-gazette.com/localcity /2009/04/13/Experts-track-the-patterns-of-mass-murders/stories /200904130098 (accessed March 2, 2016).

Chapter 1: The Murderous Leaders and Followers of Family Cults

1. "Notorious Killer Who Murdered Five People in Bizarre Plot 'To Speed Christ's Return to Earth' Hangs Himself on Death Row," *The Daily Mail*, April 16, 2013, http://www.dailymail.co.uk/news/article-2309952 /Justin-Helzer-case-Notorious-killer-murdered-people-bizarre-plot -speed-Christs-return-Earth-hangs-death-row.html (accessed January 26, 2016).
2. Cynthia Stalter Sasse and Peggy Murphy Widder, *The Kirtland Massacre* (New York: Zebra Books, 1992), p. 25, 31.
3. "Murderer Who Said He Was Prophet Is Executed," NBC News, October 25, 2006, http://www.nbcnews.com/id/15398559/ns/us_news -crime_and_courts/t/murderer-who-said-he-was-prophet-executed /#.VqgYSlMrIyk (accessed January 26, 2016).
4. Josh Gardner, "Utah Couple Became Obsessed With Killer Polygamist Cult Leader and Visited Him in Jail Before Poisoning Themselves and Their Kids," *The Daily Mail*, January 28, 2015, http://www.dailymail.co.uk /news/article-2929451/Utah-parents-showed-troubling-signs-deaths .html (accessed October 16, 2015).
5. Nuel Emmons, *Manson In His Own Words* (New York: Grove Press, 1988).
6. Janet Maslin, "Long Before Little Charlie Became the Face of Evil," *New York Times*, August 6, 2013, http://www.nytimes.com/2013/08/07 /books/a-new-look-at-charles-manson-by-jeff-guinn.html?_r=0 (accessed January 28, 2016).
7. Vincent Bugliosi and Curt Gentry, *Helter Skelter: The True Story of the Manson Murders* (New York: W.W. Norton & Company, 1974).

117

Chapter 2: The Murderous Leaders and Followers of Occult and Satanic Cults

1. Robert Reinhold, "The Longest Trial—A Post-Mortem; Collapse of Child Abuse Case: So Much Agony for So Little," *New York Times*, January 24, 1990, http://www.nytimes.com/1990/01/24/us/longest-trial-post-mortem-collapse-child-abuse-case-so-much-agony-for-so-little.html (accessed January 25, 2016).

2. Kenneth Lanning, "1992 FBI Report- Satanic Ritual Abuse," CultWatch, http://www.cultwatch.com/satanicabuse.html (accessed October 25, 2015).

3. Charlotte Greig, *Evil Serial Killers: In the Minds of Monsters* (New York: Barnes & Noble, 2006), p. 88.

4. Michael Newton, *Hunting Humans: An Encyclopedia of Modern Serial Killers* (Port Townsend, WA.: Loompanics Unlimited, 1990).

5. Ibid.

6. Jennifer Vigil, "Rapist's Son Is Among 3 Charged in Slaying," *Chicago Tribune,* March 7, 1999, http://articles.chicagotribune.com/1999-03-07/news/9903070261_1_slaying-northwest-side-john-wayne-gacy (accessed October 25, 2015).

7. Philip Carlo, *The Night Stalker: The Life and Crimes of Richard Ramirez* (New York: Kensington Publishing Corp, 1996).

8. Anthony Bruno, "The Night Stalker: Satanists Don't Wear Gold (The Marriage of Richard Ramirez and Doreen Lioy)," *Crime Library*, TruTV, 2011, Turner Entertainment Networks, Inc.

9. Al Baker, "Band Member Leads Police Cult to Killings," *Sun Sentinel,* June 21, 2004, http://articles.sun-sentinel.com/2004-06-21/news/0406200242_1_band-members-killings-satan (accessed October 26, 2015).

10. Ibid.

Chapter 3: The Murderous Leaders and Followers of Religious Cults

1. Christopher Smith, "Scientology's Money Trail," *Entrepreneur*, December 8, 2008, http://www.entrepreneur.com/article/199106 (accessed January 26, 2016).
2. George Chryssides, *Come On Up and I Will Show Thee': Heaven's Gate as a Postmodern Group* (Oxford University Press, 2005).
3. Robert Balch and David Taylor, *Making Sense of the Heaven's Gate Suicides* (Cambridge University Press, 2002).
4. Ibid.
5. "Heaven's Gate: A Timeline," *San Diego Union-Tribune*, March 18, 2007, http://www.utsandiego.com/uniontrib/20070318/news_lz1n18timelin .html (accessed November 2, 2015).
6. "Swamiji's Life Story," Swami Premananda Official Website, http:// sripremananda.org/teachings/swamijis-life-story/ (accessed November 2, 2015).
7. Ben Bradlee Jr. and Dale Van Atta, *Prophet of Blood: The Untold Story of Ervil LeBaron and the Lambs of God* (New York: G.G. Putnam's Sons, 1981).
8. Biography.com editors, "Joseph Di Mambro Biography." Biography.com. http://www.biography.com/people/joseph-di-mambro-235990#cult -founder (accessed November 4, 2015).

Chapter 4: The Murderous Leaders and Followers of Doomsday Cults

1. Patrick Ajuna, "Did Kibwetere Die in Inferno?" *New Vision*, March 20, 2013, http://www.newvision.co.ug/new_vision/news/1315913 /kibwetere-die-inferno (accessed November 13, 2015).
2. Stephen Atkins, *Encyclopedia of Modern Worldwide Extremists and Extremist Groups* (Westport, CT: Greenwood Press, 2004), p. 27.
3. Jennifer Latson, "How a Religious Sect Rooted in Yoga Became a Terrorist Group," *Time*, March 20, 2015, http://time.com/3742241/tokyo -subway-attack-1995/ (accessed January 30, 2016).

4. Colin Wilson, *The Devil's Party* (London, England: Virgin Books, 2000).

5. Eugene Gallagher and James Tabor, *Why Waco? Cults and the Battle for Religious Freedom in America* (Los Angeles: University of California Press, 1995), p. 18.

6. "Frequently Asked Questions About Waco," PBS, http://www.pbs.org /wgbh/pages/frontline/waco/topten.html (accessed November 21, 2015).

Chapter 5: The Murderous Leaders and Followers of Political and Terrorist Cults

1. John J. Wilson, "Preventing Adolescent Gang Involvement," U.S. Department of Justice, September 2000, https://www.ncjrs.gov/pdffiles1 /ojjdp/182210.pdf (accessed January 31, 2016).

2. "Timeline: Osama bin Laden's Life History," *The Telegraph*, May 2, 2012, http://www.telegraph.co.uk/news/worldnews/asia/pakistan/9240249 / Timeline-Osama-bin-Ladens-life-history.html (accessed December 2, 2015).

3. Ibid.

4. "Marxism-Leninism," *New World Encyclopedia*, http://www .newworldencyclopedia.org/entry/Marxism-Leninism (accessed December 2, 2015).

5. "Truth Commission: Peru 01," United States Institute of Peace, http://www .usip.org/publications/truth-commission-peru-01 (accessed December 3, 2015).

6. "Shining Path Militant Leaders Given Life Sentences in Peru," CBC News, October 13, 2006, http://www.cbc.ca/news/world/shining-path-militant -leaders-given-life-sentences-in-peru-1.628864 (accessed December 5, 2015).

7. Craig Whitlock, "Al-Zarqawi's Biography," *The Washington Post*, June 8, 2006, http://www.washingtonpost.com/wp-dyn/content /article/2006/06/08/AR2006060800299.html?nav=rss_world/africa (accessed December 6, 2015).

8. Craig Whitlock, "Zarqawi Building His Own Terror Network," *Pittsburgh Post-Gazette*, October 3, 2004, http://old.post-gazette.com /pg/04277/388966.stm (accessed December 6, 2015).
9. Craig Whitlock, "Death Could Shake Al-Qaeda in Iraq and Around the World," *The Washington Post*, June 10, 2006, http://www.washingtonpost .com/wp-dyn/content/article/2006/06/09/AR2006060902040.html (accessed December 7, 2015).

Conclusion

1. Paul Mountjoy, "The Disturbing Revelations of a Now Engaged Charles Manson," *Communities Digital News*, November 18, 2014, http://www .commdiginews.com/health-science/health/the-disturbing-revelations -of-a-now-engaged-charles-manson-29979/ (accessed January 31, 2016).
2. "Brothers Tell of Surviving Cult," *Religion News Blog*, October 6, 2010, http://www.religionnewsblog.com/25186/brothers-tell-of-surviving-cult (accessed January 31, 2016).

allegation—An assertion or pronouncement made without hard proof.

apocalypticism—The religious belief that the world will soon come to an end.

assassination—The act of destroying something—usually a person—viciously, suddenly, or secretly.

authoritarian control—The exercising of complete control over an individual.

cult—A group of people who are devoted to a person, an idea, an object, a movement, or a work.

doomsday—A day of judgment or sentence, sometimes signaling the end of the world.

indicted—The act of officially being charged with an offense or crime by a grand jury.

jihad—A holy Islamic war accepted as a Muslim duty.

manipulation—The handling and management of an individual in a way that gets them to do what you want.

Marian apparition—A supernatural appearance of the Blessed Virgin Mary.

monasticism—A religious way of life in which a person puts their own personal life aside in order to devote themselves to their religion or spiritual work.

nganga—A spiritual healer or herbalist that's derived from African societies; also a type of cauldron.

occult—Supernatural or magical beliefs or practices.

psychological abuse—A type of abuse characterized by a person being subjected to negative behavior of the mind, including anxiety, depression, and post-traumatic stress disorder.

ritual—A repetitive act or common actions that usually involve a religious ceremony.

sleeper cell—An organization of terrorists who are planted within a secret area and told not to strike until their leader tells them to.

worship—The act of adoring or admiring an individual, in some cases a religious figure.

Further Reading

Books

Guinn, Jeff. Manson: *The Life and Times of Charles Manson.* New York: Simon & Schuster, 2014.

Latta, Sara. *Medical Serial Killers.* New York: Enslow Publishing, 2016.

Rauf, Don. *Female Serial Killers.* New York: Enslow Publishing, 2016.

Steiger, Brad, and Sherry Steiger. *Conspiracies and Secret Societies: The Complete Dossier.* Canton, MI: Visible Ink Press, 2012.

Tibbott, Julie. *Members Only: Secret Societies, Sects, and Cults Exposed!* San Francisco: Zest Books, 2015.

Woog, Adam. *Careers in the FBI.* New York: Cavendish Square, 2014.

Websites

FBI Kids
fbi.gov/fun-games/kids
The FBI Kids website is an interactive way for students to learn more about the activities, mission, and purpose of the FBI.

Murderpedia.org
murderpedia.org/
This encyclopedia contains biographies of murderers.

Psychology Today
psychologytoday.com/blog/wicked-deeds/201407/ why-spree-killers-are-not-serial-killers
Read about the difference between spree killers and serial killers.

Movies

Ambush in Waco: In the Line of Duty (TV movie), 1993.
Helter Skelter (TV movie), 2004.

Index

About the Author

Pete Schauer is a professional writer and digital marketer, holding a BA in English Writing and an MA in Professional Communication from William Paterson University. His writing experience stems from his time with Bleacher Report, Rosen Publishing, and most recently, Social Media Today. Pete lives in New Jersey with his wife, Liz, and their dog, Toby.